25th April, 2016

Go
O

Justice

By Eric Mumford

P.O. Box 3709 ❖ Cookeville, TN 38502
931.520.3730 ❖ lc@lifechangers.org

PLUMBLINE

Published by:

LIBRARY SERIES

P.O. Box 3709 | Cookeville, TN 38502
(800) 521-5676 | www.lifechangers.org

God Magnified, Part 10
Observing Coequality and Jusice

Contents

God Magnified, Part 10
Observing Coequality and Justice

By Eric Mumford

Introduction: God Magnified

God is an "**Us**" (Gen. 1:26, 3:22, 11:7; Isa. 6:8).

"God is **one**" (Deut. 6:4; Mark 12:29).

"God is **Agape**" (1John 4:8, 16).

"God is a **sun**" (Ps. 84:11).

"**Holy, Holy, Holy** is the Lord God, the **Almighty**" (Rev. 4:8; Isa. 6:8).

"God is **Light**" (1John 1:5).

"The eternal God is a **dwelling place**" (Deut. 33:27).

God is "**in Christ**" (Col. 2:9; 2 Cor. 5:19; Eph. 4:32).

"God is **Spirit**" (John 4:24).

"God is **true**" (John 3:33).

God is "**Most High**" (Ps. 57:2; Acts 7:48).

"The Lord is a God of **justice**" (Isa. 30:18).

"The Lord, whose name is *Jealous*, is a **jealous** God" (Ex. 34:14).

"God is a **consuming fire**" (Deut. 4:24; Heb. 12:29).

God is three **sacrificial Self-sharers**

The "*God is*" statements of the Scriptures are like pillars of a covered porch built around the entire circumference of **the kingdom of God:** "God is a dwelling place." Each pillar serves as a lens to see and understand the next. Progressive magnification of these statements leads to a three-dimensional understanding of this eternal cohabitation and draws us to enter and participate as *self-sharers,* through the God-Man Jesus, in the "eternal life" of Father, Son, and Spirit. As emigrants to the kingdom, we are pioneering forward together into this unfolding revelation of **the fusion of the Trinity**.

In the previous volume, *God Magnified Part 9: Abiding in "The Lord of hosts"*, we learned that our Triune-God is profoundly inclusive and hospitable. Through the Spirit, the Son Jesus prayed to Father for you and me, saying, **"that they may be in Us**...that they may be one, just as We are one" (John 17:21-22). These three, eternal Self-sharers have purposed to include us in Their own relational fusion and inter-personal oneness, which is "the kingdom of God" (Luke 6:20). As a Host, the Trinity has invited "hosts" of unique individuals to cohabit with Them in the combined and combining God-Man Jesus Christ who 'embodies' within Himself this shared kingdom.

The '**blueprints**' of the relational, inter-personal infrastructure of "the Lord of hosts" are illustrated through the Scriptures in various, creative ways. We examined these blueprints **from macro to micro:** 1. individual "**stars**" encompass the nucleus of one galaxy and move together in the swirling arms of this vortex; 2. individual, unlocked "**gardens**" adjoin one another and become one shared estate; 3. "**living stones**" are fit together on one Cornerstone and become one building; and 4. individual "**members**" are incorporated into the one body (corpus) of one Man, Christ Jesus.

In the previous volume, we recognized that Father, Son, and Spirit, as sacrificial Self-sharers, do not have an inheritance to give 'me' as an autonomous **proprietor**; the only inheritance They have to give is 'a share' in Their one shared estate. The Persons of our Triune-God **steward** "all things" on behalf of One Another and on our behalf as "heirs of God and fellow heirs with Christ" (Rom. 8:17). Father, Son, and Spirit are '**Shareholders**' of this one, fruit-bearing estate, a Family 'business' of bountiful *gene-rosity*, a '**corporation**' into which these Three are *Themselves* **incorporated**. As Self-sharers, the Triune-God of *Agape* desires for human beings to become shareholders with Them; therefore, They made Their own *private* Family 'business' a *public* corporation by relocating "all the fullness" of Their shared estate into the **corpus** of the God-Man Jesus Christ: "For in Christ all the fullness of Deity [*Father, Son, Spirit*] dwells in **bodily form**, and in Him [*incorporated into the God-Man*] you have been made full" (Col. 2:9-10).

All human beings have been invited to believe into (*buy into*) "God in Christ"—forfeiting their own autonomous lives to be **incorporated** (fused) as sacrificial self-sharing "members" of Jesus' own resurrected **corpus** (many-membered body). In the first church, followers of Jesus were incorporated into the kingdom of God as Trinity-like shareholders: "And the congregation of those who believed were of **one heart and soul** [*Trinity-like*]; and not one [*individual*] of them claimed that anything belonging to him was **his own** [*forfeiting autonomy, individualism, proprietorship*], but all things were **common property to them** [*one shared life*]" (Acts 4:32).

In the previous volume, we also examined the blueprints of the cohabitation of the kingdom illustrated in another way: this one shared estate is comprised of **unlocked, adjoining gardens**. As a prophetic type of Christ the Bridegroom and us, His many-membered bride, Solomon wrote, "**A garden locked** is my sister, my bride, **a rock garden locked** [*in eros individualism: self-worth-ship, self-preservation*]" (Song 4:12). God has given each one of us the gift of individuality and free will: my own mind, my own heart, my own life (nucleus)—**my own "garden."** As an immature believer, I am still largely tyrannized by self-worth-ship; therefore, I spend all my time cultivating my garden *for* 'me.' I only invite into my garden those whom I calculate will add to me. Those I estimate to be a liability I intentionally shut out. Hardened in self-interest, I am "a rock garden locked."

The kingdom of our Triune-God remains eclipsed to those who seek to preserve their own "garden" in **individualism**: "For whoever wishes to **save his life** [*e.g. his own garden*] will lose it [*fission decay*]; but whoever loses his life [*as a sacrificial self-sharer*] for My sake [*into the God-Man Nucleus*] will find it [*fused into the cohabitation of the Trinity and man: 'one shared estate'*]" (Matt. 16:25). Jesus Himself used this analogy of the garden:

> Jesus was saying, "What is the **kingdom of God** [*three Self-sharers*] like, and to what shall I compare it? It is like a mustard **seed** [*fuse-able DNA*] that a man [*individual*] took and threw into **his own garden** [*autonomous life*], and it grew and became a tree, and the birds of every wing nested in its branches [*inclusive hospitality*]" (Luke 13:18-19).

Father, Son, and Spirit, as free, Self-sharing Individuals, live eternally in One Another's **open, adjoining gardens** (mutual indwelling); therefore, "God is a dwelling place" (Deut. 33:27). According to these relational 'blueprints,' the unlocked, open garden of each individual human being **adjoins** the unlocked gardens of other kingdom sons and daughters and becomes one shared estate: "behold, the kingdom of God is in your midst" (Luke 17:21). Our Triune-God does not merely want to live in us as individuals, but in the one shared estate of **our adjoining** (fused) **lives!**

Now, in this *God Magnified* volume, we will magnify the eleventh pillar—"**the Lord is a God of justice**" (Isa. 30:18). We discover why sacrificial self-sharing and justice are one, inseparable reality rooted in the very nature our Triune-Creator as Coequals. Sacrificial self-sharing (mature Agape) constitutes "the law" of our Triune-God and the bedrock of true justice, which **preserves freedom and coequality** among all those individuals who enter and participate together in the kingdom of God. Justice is a redemptive manifestation of the Presence of the Trinity that exposes, confronts, and corrects our **incapacity to share**. In other words, the law of Agape and Triune-Justice ensure that each of us behaves in a proper, godly (Trinity-like) manner while we are 'in' one another's unlocked, open gardens! Paul wrote:

> That you will know **how one** [*individual*] **ought to conduct himself in the household of God** [*cohabitation of the Trinity and human beings*], which is the church [*many-membered corpus*] of the living, **the pillar and support of the truth** [*the created 'us' manifesting the Agape of the eternal "Us"*] (1 Tim. 3:15).

1. The Eternal Root of Coequality and Justice

As we magnify the "*God is*" statements of the Scriptures individually and collectively, we discover they illumine the Root-Source of literally every thing that affects our practical, daily lives: all the sciences, philosophy, mathematics, engineering, architecture and all the various arts (*in-gen-uity*), education, psychology, sociology, economics, and government, as well as **the foundation of law and justice**. Though our Triune-Creator (the "Us") is the Architect of all that exists, God is *not* the author of the counterfeits and perversions that Satan (Worthless) and *de-gene-rate* mankind have introduced into creation by "**devising evil**" (Ps. 140:2; Hos. 7:15; Acts 4:25).

The previous *God Magnified* volumes have helped us to **distinguish between *eros*** (self-love, self-worth-ship) **and *Agape*** (sacrificial self-giving/sharing love): self-consciousness *versus* self-forgetfulness; self-indulgence *vs* self-emptying; de-gene-rate takers *vs* gene-rous givers; self-preservation *vs* losing (laying down) one's own life; relational fission *vs* relational fusion; **the darkness** of individualism *vs* **the Light** of individuals in oneness; unholy (the living dead) *vs* holy (the dead living); **the lie** (egoism) versus **the truth** (altruism); jealousy-of *vs* jealousy-for; worthless (counterfeit) *vs* precious (gen-uine); buying/selling *vs* giving/receiving; ownership *vs* stewardship; the movement of self-exaltation: **upward descent** *vs* the movement of self-emptying humility: **downward ascent**.

There is yet another aspect of "the divine nature," along with its antithesis, which the Scriptures reference hundreds of times because it is *essential* to a true knowledge and holistic understanding of our Triune-God: "**justice**" and "**injustice**" also referred to as "**lawful**" and "**lawless**." Each of us was born with a de-gene-rate, *lawless* nature. In varying degrees of practice, skill, and maturity, we are all 'takers' with an innate aversion to sharing. As we magnify the eternal Root and Source of Justice, "The Lord is a God of Justice" (Isa. 30:18), we discover Father, Son, and Spirit, as *gene-rous* Self-sharers and Coequals, are *Themselves* **the solution to our incapacity to share**. The prophet Isaiah who "saw the Lord…Holy, Holy, Holy" also saw the God of justice:

Therefore the Lord longs to be **gracious** to you, and therefore He waits on high to have **compassion** on you [*e.g. God Most High, three who mutually exalt One Another, seek to lift fallen mankind into Themselves*]. For **the Lord is a God of justice** [*lit. Heb.: mishpat—act of deciding a case*]; how blessed are all those who long for Him [*e.g. Agape magnetism: reciprocal self-sharing love*]. O people in Zion [*cohabitation of the kingdom*], **inhabitant** [*individual*] **in Jerusalem**, you will weep no longer. He will surely be gracious to you at the sound of your cry; when He hears it, He will answer you.

Although the Lord has given you [*e.g. caused you to reap*] **bread of privation** [*famine: result of opportunism, self-indulgence*] and **water of oppression** [*slavery: result of buying and selling one another*], He, your Teacher [*Triune-Most*

High] will no longer hide Himself, but **your eyes will behold your Teacher** [*"Jesus, Son of the Most High God"*]. Your ears will hear a word behind you [*e.g. "the Spirit of Christ" within you*], "**This is the way** [*Trinity-likeness: freedom and equality in reciprocal self-sharing*], **walk in it**," whenever you turn to the right or to the left [*chasing mirages as an opportunist in Worthless' world*] (Isa. 30:18-21).

To keep warm, **a family of porcupines** must huddle together in one, shared burrow, yet each must learn to do so very carefully! Justice is the gift of our Triune-God to keep us warm. In any **cohabitation**—a family, team, community, nation, etc.—**justice** preserves the freedom and equality of the individuals who live and participate in it by ensuring that each individual **shares equitably** with others. "**Righteousness** [*sacrificial self-sharing*], **justice** [*law and order*], and **equity** [*equality*]" (Prov. 1:3; Ps. 33:5; Isa. 9:7; Matt. 23:23; Col. 4:1) are a 'trio' often repeated through the Scriptures because these are the fundamental components of a peaceful, fruit-bearing cohabitation.

Jesus died as the Representative "Son of Man"; He embodied within Himself all human beings who were disjointed from God and one another in relational fission: "**all My bones are out of joint**" (Ps. 22:14). Justice is God's means of keeping you, me, and all the other individual "bones" of Jesus' many-membered "body" properly jointed and in functional alignment.

The **blueprints** of a just and equitable cohabitation of free individuals originates in our **Triune-Creator** Themselves. Not only do Father, Son, and Spirit *cohabit* with One Another, these Three *mutually indwell* One Another; "the eternal God *is* a dwelling place" (Deut. 33:27). David affirmed, "A father of the fatherless and **a judge** for the widows [*vulnerable individuals*] **is God in His holy** [*eros-free*] **habitation**" (Ps. 68:5). When we carefully magnify this "holy habitation," we discover it is actually the *cohabitation* of "Holy, Holy, Holy" referred to in the Scriptures as "**the Holy** [*fusion Oneness*] **of Holies** [*three Selfless Self-sharers*]" (Heb. 9:3).

Father, Son, and Spirit are humble, Self-emptied "Holies" who mutually indwell One Another in **sacrificial Self-sharing equality—coequality**. The desert fathers observed, "**God in Himself is a sweet society** [*e.g. three Eternals who share one free, equitable, and just cohabitation*]." The Triune-God of justice was ultimately revealed in Christ Jesus who we will come to know as '*the Equalizer*', but see how justice was first revealed to David: "**God** [*Father, Son, Spirit*] **leads the humble** [*self-emptied*] **in justice** [*relational freedom and coequality*], **and He teaches the humble His way** [*reciprocal Self-sharing*]" (Ps. 25:9).

The Hebrew word for justice is *mishpat* meaning: judgment, order, deciding a case, right decisions. The only One qualified and capable of making an impartial decision—a verdict that is not corrupted by self-interest or influenced by improper loyalty—is a self-emptied self-sharer; God is a Judge. "God is not one to show **partiality**" (Acts 10:34). In many biblical accounts those who suffered injustice at the hands of a corrupt individual but had confidence in the "incorruptible God" (Rom. 1:23), would say, "May the Lord, the Judge, judge between you and me" (Gen. 16:5; Judg. 11:25; 1 Sam. 24:12).

As *de-gene-rate* individualists, tyrannized by self-worth-ship, you and I are porcupines who stab and torment one another: we do not want to share; we don't know how to share; and we are *gene-tically* and instinctually **incapable of sharing as coequals**. Having 'bought into' Worthless' *eros* nature, rationale, and economy, we buy and sell one another in mutual exploitation. Playing his 'king of the mountain' game in self-exaltation, there is no equality among us—**Injustice**. Therefore, in *Agape* the "Us" of our genesis—"a God of **justice**"—must intervene to preserve freedom and coequality among us. Man-made 'justice systems' that are not derived from a "true knowledge" of this eternal Root are perverted or, at best, grossly inadequate to achieve and maintain freedom, equality, and peace among human beings. God spoke to the prophet Jeremiah:

> Stand in the **gate** of the Lord's house [*entrance into the cohabitation of the kingdom*] and proclaim…"**Amend your ways** [*forsake eros individualism, self-worth-ship*] **and your deeds**

[*opportunism, self-indulgence*], and I will let you dwell in this place. **If you truly practice justice** [*sacrificial self-sharing: coequality*] **between a man and his neighbor**, if you do not oppress the alien, the orphan, or the widow [*exploiting or marginalizing the weaker "members"*] and do not shed innocent blood in this place, nor walk after other gods [*confusion in "the lie"*] to your own ruin [*fission decay*], **then I will let you dwell in this place** [*cohabitation of three coequal Self-sharers*]" (Jer. 7:2-7).

2. "The Perfect Law...the Royal Law"

Freedom, equality, and justice among individuals and groups of individuals could not exist or function without law. A *code of justice* defines the rules of sharing, and a *justice system* also called *law and order* interprets, applies, and enforces those rules to preserve freedom and maintain equality among individuals in each unique situation. The Scriptures describe three basic types of law:

1. The law of **Agape**, also referred to as "the law of Christ" (Gal. 6:2) and "the law of the Spirit... the law of God" (Rom. 8:2, 7)
2. "the law of **sin and death**" (Rom. 8:2)—a counterfeit and perversion of the law of Agape
3. "the Law of **Moses**" (Luke 24:44) based on the Ten Commandments.

The first two laws are *internal*, written into the nature (DNA) of an individual; the law of Moses is *external* law, written on tablets of stone. As Individuals, Father, Son, and Spirit are Themselves governed by one law: "**the whole Law is fulfilled in one word**, in Jesus' statement, 'You shall **love** [*lit. Agape*] **your neighbor as** [*e.g. in place of*] **yourself**'" (Gal. 5:14). The Scriptures clearly define and illustrate what it means to love another *in place of* yourself in the sacrificial self-sharing brotherhood of Jonathan and David who, by faith, entered into "**the covenant** [*fusion agreement: law*] **of the Lord** [*Triune-Agape: coequality*]" (1 Sam. 20:8; see 18:1-4; 20:1-23; 23:15-18).

"The eternal kingdom" (2 Pet. 1:11) existed before heaven and earth or any angelic or human beings were created: The eternal Father, the eternal Son, and the eternal Spirit are three "**neighbors**" who abide by the law of Agape so perfectly (lawfully) that They mutually indwell One Another. Not only do Father, Son, and Spirit *share* this one law and abide by it as one "incorruptible God" (Rom. 1:23), They *are* that law: "God is Agape" (1 John 4:8). Paul taught:

> Owe nothing to anyone except to love [*lit. Agape*] one another; for **he who loves** [*sacrificially shares himself with*] **his neighbor** [*as his coequal*] **has fulfilled the law** [*of Father, Son, and Spirit: three Coequals*]....Love [*lit. Agape*] does no wrong [*opportunism, usury*] to

a neighbor; therefore **love** [*lit. Agape: sacrificial self-sharing*] **is the fulfillment of the law** [*of the incorruptible Triune-God*] (Rom. 13:8-10).

James referred to Agape as "**the perfect** [*lit. telios: mature; incorruptible*] **law, the law of liberty…the royal law** [*lit. the law of our King*]" (James 1:23; 2:8). The law of Agape is not a 'code' of rules that Father, Son, and Spirit decided to design, develop, and perfect. Rather, the law of Agape is uncreated—'written' into **the inward nature** (DNA) of each Person of the **Trinity** as an eternal Being. Agape is Who these three, unique Self-sharers *are* by nature—a DNA-match— "the Lord is a God of justice."

According to this **internal law of extraverted gene-rosity**, each of the three Persons of the Trinity *humbles* Himself to *exalt* the other Two, and each *empties* Himself to *add* to the other Two. None of the Three uses or exploits the other Two, and each of the Three sacrificially *forsakes* Himself for the *sake* of the other Two who are His eternal Beloved. Bob Mumford declared, "**Agape is the only absolute I know**." The one and only root-source of true justice is *Who* these three "incorruptible" Eternals *are* individually and as one. Apart from seeing, knowing, and worth-shipping our Triune-Creator, it is impossible for us to implement true justice among ourselves—**law-full-ness is Trinity-likeness**.

As a personal confession, Paul described another *internal* law:

For we know that the Law is spiritual, but I am of flesh [*de-gene-rate*], sold into bondage to sin [*eros, corruption*]. For what I am doing, I do not understand; for I am not practicing what I would like to do [*self-sharing*], but I am doing the very thing I hate [*self-indulgence*]. But if I do the very thing I do not want to do, I agree with the Law, confessing that the Law is good....For I know that nothing good dwells in me, that is, in my flesh; for the willing is present in me, but the doing of the good [*lawfulness*] is not. For the good that I want, I do not do, but I practice the very evil [*lawlessness*] that I do not want. But if I am doing the very thing I do not want, I [*the individual*] am no longer the one doing it, but sin [*eros individualism*] which dwells in me.

I find then the principle that evil is present in me, the one who wants to do good. For I joyfully concur with **the law of God** [*Agape*] in the inner man [*DNA*], **but I see a different law** [*counterfeit*] in the members of my body, waging war against the law of my mind [*conscience*] and making me a prisoner of **the law of sin** [*eros: compulsive, self-indulgent nature*] which is in my members. Wretched man that I am! Who will set me free from the body of this **death** [*corruption, fission decay*]? (Rom. 7:23-24).

The inhumanity of man to man is a manifestation of the *de-gene-rate*, beastly, lawless nature we have in common with the false-father Worthless. This "law" at work within all of Adam's offspring is an *internal* compulsion contrary to the law of Agape that causes us, individually and as a society, to mature in "the lie," practice opportunism, and *de-gene-rate* into corruption. Though the fruit of this law is "lawlessness," sin is called a "law" because it governs and rules the nature, rationale, and behavior of human beings.

Before God came among men in the Person of Christ, God gave the people of Israel "the Law of Moses" to keep them from devouring and consuming one another in unrestrained lawlessness. It is truly said, "**Rules are all that keep us from a dog-eat-dog world.**" On Mount Sinai, "the Lord spoke to Moses, 'Go down at once, for your people…have corrupted themselves. They have quickly turned aside from the way which I commanded them. They have made for themselves a molten calf.'…Moses saw that the people were **out of control** [*lit. let loose; casting off restraint; lawless*]" (Ex. 32:7-8; 25).

The Law of Moses is different from the *internal* law of Agape and the *internal* law of sin and death because it is an *external* law, "written on tablets of stone" (2 Cor. 3:3)—*outside* of man. Corruption, lawlessness, opportunism, and inhumanity are curbed, tamed, and held in check most of the time in our families and communities by '**law and order**,' or more precisely, by **threat of punishment:** fear of penalty, humiliation, and personal loss. In self-interest and self-preservation, I 'calculate' the risk of suffering punishment is not worth the gratification (potential payoff) of committing the lawless, self-indulgent act.

However, there are not **external laws** strong enough to make us simply renounce our default-mode of individualism, forsake our lawless habits, and cease opportunism and exploitation of one another. The compulsive, eros nature—"the law of sin"—continues to rule us from within. In our de-gene-rate state, all men are "**slaves of sin…slaves to impurity and to lawlessness**" (Rom. 6:17-19).

Serving as a steward of the Fatherhood of God to 26 American, Ukrainian, and Ugandan children thus far has helped me understand how effectively the *internal* law of sin works against *external* family rules! A store manager wrote the following employee evaluation: "He works well…when he is cornered like a rat in a trap!" The twisted, crafty, serpent-like nature of the false-father in the people of Israel found ways around these *external* laws of God to exploit one another for self-indulgence. Jesus said, "Woe to you, scribes and Pharisees, hypocrites, because you **devour widows' houses**, and for a pretense you make long prayers; therefore you will receive greater condemnation" (Matt. 23:14). Our Triune-God anticipated our wayward, corruptible, lawless nature and prepared a solution:

For on the one hand, there is a setting aside of a **former commandment** because of its weakness and uselessness, for **the Law** [*e.g. Moses' external law*] **made nothing perfect** [*telios: mature in Agape: God's sacrificial self-sharing DNA*], and on the other hand there is a bringing in of **a better hope** [*"Christ in you, the hope of glory" Col. 1:27*], through which we draw near to God [*participate in the cohabitation of three Self-sharers*].... "For this is the **covenant** [*fusion agreement*] I will make with the house of Israel after those days [*after the coming of Christ*]," says the Lord: "**I will put My laws into their minds** [*Agape rationale*], **and I will write them on their hearts** [*just as it is written into the DNA of the Trinity*].

And I will be their God, and they shall be My people [*gen-uine sons and daughters of the Lord God of hosts*]. And they shall not teach everyone his **fellow citizen** [*sharers of one cohabitation*], and everyone his brother, saying, 'Know the Lord,' for **all will know Me** [*Triune-Agape*], from the least to the greatest of them. For I will be merciful to their iniquities, and I will remember their sins no more [*e.g. criminal records expunged*]." When He said, "**A new covenant**," He has made the first [*Moses' external law*] obsolete. But whatever is becoming obsolete and growing old is ready to disappear (Heb. 7:18-19; 8:10-13).

If the Law of Moses proved to be weak and useless to "perfect" human beings as sacrificial self-sharers (e.g. re-gene-rate de-gene-rate men), why then did God give this Law? Human beings are tyrannized by self-worth-ship and self-will. To prepare us to empty ourselves that we might humbly receive a Savior and His communicable nature of Agape as a gift, it was necessary for God to afford us time to discover we were **entirely incapable of keeping the Law**. It was necessary to demonstrate that every attempt at self-righteousness and self-salvation would fail and prove utterly "futile" (Rom. 8:20-21).

One who considers himself to be a self-sufficient, self-made man will never ask God to do for him what he believes he can do for himself! When self-willed men come to the end of themselves, then "perhaps God may **grant them repentance** leading to the knowledge of the truth [*Triune-Agape*], and they may come to their senses [*awaken from "the lie": eros rationale*] and **escape from the snare of the devil** [*the law of sin and death*], having been held captive by him to do his will" (2 Tim. 2:25-26).

Further, the Law of Moses served as an elementary primer to awaken self-conscious human beings, like spoiled, contentious children, to their self-centered condition and the cruel impact that self-indulgence has on one's neighbors: "But if there is any further injury, then you shall appoint as a **penalty** life for life, eye for eye, tooth for tooth, hand for hand, foot for foot, burn for burn, wound for wound, bruise for bruise" (Ex. 21:23-25). Paul explained it this way:

> Therefore **the Law** [*e.g. Moses' external law*] **has become our tutor** [*lit. padeia: education in discipline and wisdom*] **to lead us to Christ** [*the perfect Prototype Man*], so that we may be justified by faith [*seeing and buying into three Self-sharers revealed in Christ*]. But now that faith has come [*by which we receive the seed of Agape DNA: re-gene-ration in God's internal law*], we are no longer under a tutor [*external law*] (Gal. 3:24-25).

A cohabitation of freedom, coequality, justice, and relational harmony is the fruit of the law of Agape within each individual—an expression of the divine nature, the very DNA of our Triune-Creator "**written not with ink but with the Spirit of the living God, not on tablets of stone but on tablets of human hearts**" (2 Cor. 3:3).

According to man's self-referential interpretation of the *external* Law of Moses, *lawfulness* is motivated by two things: securing a blessing for 'me' and avoiding the punishment of 'me'. Both motivations are **self-serving** and promote introspection, hypocrisy, and an exacting, judgmental spirit. According to the *internal* law of Agape, *lawfulness* is motivated purely by **conscious concern for others,** which promotes self-forgetfulness, self-sharing, and compassion. See how the law of Christ transcends Moses' Law:

> Unless your righteousness surpasses that of the scribes and Pharisees [*experts in Mosaic Law*], you will not enter the kingdom of heaven [*a cohabitation of self-sharing coequals*]....You have heard that it was said, "An eye for an eye, and a tooth for a tooth." But I say to you, **do not resist an evil person**; but whoever slaps you on your right cheek, turn the other to him also. If anyone wants to sue you and take your shirt, let him have your coat also. Whoever forces you to go one mile, go with him two. **Give to him who asks of you**, and do not turn away from him who wants to borrow from you.

> You have heard that it was said, "You shall love your neighbor and hate your enemy." But I say to you, **love your enemies** and pray for those who persecute you, so that you may be [*gen-uine*] sons of your [*gene-rous*] Father who is in heaven; for He causes His sun to rise on the evil and the good, and sends rain on the righteous and the unrighteous....Therefore **you are to be perfect** [*lit. telios: a mature sacrificial self-sharer*], **as your heavenly Father is perfect** (Matt. 5:20; 38-48).

Due to a self-referential interpretation of the Law of Moses, the religious Jews became so eclipsed in self-focus and enslaved in self-righteousness that it was very difficult for them to understand and embrace the burden-bearing law of Christ. Jesus said to them, "You are experts at setting aside the commandment of God [*e.g. coequality in Agape*] in order to keep your tradition" (Mark 7:9). As immature Christians and half-formed children, are we not caught in this very same snare?

> A ruler questioned Him, saying, "Good Teacher, **what shall I do to inherit eternal life** [*e.g. for 'me'*]**?**" And Jesus said to him, "Why do you call Me good? No one is good except God alone. You know the commandments, 'Do not commit adultery, Do not murder, Do not steal, Do not bear false witness, Honor your father and mother.'" And he said, "All these things [*Moses' external Law*] I have kept from my youth." When Jesus heard this, He said to him, "**One thing you still lack** [*e.g. you must fulfill the law of Agape: sacrificial self-sharing*]; **sell all that you possess** [*dismantle your autonomous life*] **and distribute it to the poor** [*as coequals*], and you shall have **treasure in heaven** [*a share in the life of three Self-sharers—three 'Distributors'*]; and come, **follow Me.**"

But when he had heard these things, he became very sad, for he was extremely rich. And Jesus looked at him and said, "How hard it is for those who are wealthy [*i.e. self-sufficient in self-worth*] to enter the kingdom of God [*cohabitation of self-emptied self-sharers*]! For it is easier for a camel to go through the eye of a needle than for a rich man to enter the kingdom of God [*"lose his life" into the corpus of Christ*]" (Luke 18:18-25).

The law of Agape "written" by the Spirit into the very nature and DNA of a human being *re-gene-rates* both the heart (affections) and the mind (rationale). See how Agape transforms our thinking:

The righteous [*a sacrificial self-sharer*] **is concerned for** [*lit. knows the cause of*] **the rights of the poor** [*jealous-for the freedom and coequality of others*]; **the wicked man** [*a lawless opportunist ruled by self-worth-ship and eros rationale*] **does not understand such concern** [*lit. knowledge; the Light of Agape rationale]* (Prov. 29:7).

For further understanding of how the *internal* law of Agape requires more than Moses' *external* law, meditate on Isaiah 58:1-14. Now, see how Paul identified all three kinds of "law" in Romans 8:1-9:

There is now no condemnation [*or fear of punishment*] for those who are in Christ Jesus. For **the law of the Spirit of life** [*Agape: sacrificial self-sharing*] **in Christ Jesus** has set you free from **the law of sin and of death** [*eros: individualism, corruption, fission*]. For what **the Law** [*of Moses*] could not do, weak as it was through the flesh [*human corruption*], God did: sending His own Son in the likeness of sinful flesh and as an offering for sin, He condemned sin [*eros: self-worth-ship, self-will, self-indulgence*] in the flesh, so that **the requirement of the Law** [*Moses' external Law*] **might be fulfilled <u>in</u> us** [*who are actively re-gene-rating in Agape as sacrificial self-sharers*], who do not walk according to the flesh but according to the Spirit [*e.g. in the fusion dynamic of relational oneness*].

For those who are according to the flesh [*de-gene-rate, lawless*] set their minds on the things of the flesh [*e.g. I want, I will have, I deserve to have*], but those who are according to the Spirit, the things of the Spirit [*e.g. laying down my life for the many-membered corpus*]. For the mind set on the flesh is death [*corruption: fission decay*], but the mind set on the Spirit is life and peace [*re-gene-ration: relational fusion*], because **the mind set on the flesh is hostile toward God; for it does not subject**

itself to the law of God, for it is not even able to do so [*ruled by a de-gene-rate nature, lawless instinct*], and those who are in the flesh cannot please God [*Triune-Agape*]. However, you are not in the flesh but in the Spirit, if indeed the Spirit of God [*the Re-gene-rator*] dwells in you (Rom. 8:1-9).

John stated simply and concisely how the Triune-God makes you and I sharers of Their own law: "**This is God's commandment** [*the law of three Self-sharers*], **that we believe in the name of His Son Jesus Christ** [*'buy into' the God-Man Nucleus at the 'cost' of our own autonomous lives*], **and Agape one another** [*share one name and one life as coequals in His one body*]" (1 John 3:23). The eternal Son of God *became* the Man Jesus Christ, and Father and Spirit intentionally and comprehensively **relocated into Him** (see John 1:32; 10:30; Col. 1:19; 2:9-10). According to the law of Agape, these three sacrificial Self-sharers *Themselves* fulfilled this "commandment" by fusing together into the Nucleus of a Man—"**God in Christ**" (Col. 2:9; 2 Cor. 5:19; Eph. 4:32).

Now, Father, Son, and Spirit command us individual human beings to observe and abide by Their own law—to do *exactly* what They have done— that God and human beings may cohabit together: "that they may be in Us" (John 17:21). In Trinity-likeness, we are called to **relocate into Christ** and fuse together as "members" of the one body by *lawfully* practicing the same sacrificial self-sharing Love. "Bear one another's burdens and so fulfill the law of Christ" (Gal. 6:2). Dietrich Bonhoeffer explained:

> Thus the law of Christ is a **law of bearing**. Bearing means forbearing and sustaining [*by self-expenditure*].... For the pagan, the other person never becomes a burden at all. He simply sidesteps every burden that others may impose on him. The Christian, however, must bear the burden of a brother. He must **suffer and endure the brother**. It is only when he is a burden that another person is really a brother and not merely an object to be manipulated. The burden of men was so heavy for God Himself that He had to endure the Cross. God verily bore the burden of men in the body of Jesus Christ. But He bore them as a mother carries her child....

> God took men upon Himself and they weighted Him to the ground, but God remained with them and they with God. In bearing with men, God maintained fellowship with them [*"maintaining the same Agape" Phil. 2:2*]. It is the law of Christ [*the royal law of three burden-Bearers*] that was fulfilled in the Cross. And **Christians must share in this law; they must suffer their brethren** [*as coequals*], but, what is more important, now that the law of

Christ has been fulfilled [*in a Prototype Man: a perfected Self-sharer*], they *can* bear with their brethren…. It is the fellowship of the Cross [*co-crucifixion*] to experience the burden of the other. If one does not experience it, the fellowship he belongs to is not Christian. If any member refuses to **bear that burden**, he denies the law of Christ (Bonhoeffer, *Life Together*, p. 100-101).

The law of Agape is not enforced *externally*—by police, witnesses, prosecutors, and judges. No form of **law-enforcement** can *make* you volitionally and sacrificially bear another's burden! Agape governs *internally*, from the new, re-gene-rated nature (seed) of Christ, which the Spirit cultivates within us as a new disposition: "the Agape of Christ **controls** us [*lit. holds us together*]" (2 Cor. 5:14). Apart from the law of Agape implanted as a "seed" within, the instinctual impulses of our de-gene-rate nature compel us, by default, to practice *law-lessness*. As an opportunist, I *practice* using Agape with hypocrisy to lure, deceive, and exploit you for the purpose of self-indulgence.

Everyone who **practices sin** [*eros individualism: self-worth-ship, self-will, self-indulgence*] also **practices lawlessness**; and **sin is lawlessness**. You know that He [*God in Christ*] appeared in order to take away sins; and in Him there is no sin [*individualism, self-worth-ship*]. No one who abides in Him [*in fusion in the Nucleus of Christ*] sins; no one who sins [*practices self-indulgence*] has seen Him or knows Him [*three Self-sharers revealed in Christ*]. Little children, make sure no one deceives you; the one who **practices righteousness** [*sacrificial self-sharing love*] is righteous, just as He [*the Triune-God in Christ*] is righteous; the one who practices sin is of the devil [*Worthless; de-gene-rate*]; for the devil has sinned [*practiced self-worth-ship, opportunism*] from the beginning.

The Son of God appeared for this purpose, to destroy the works of the devil [*e.g. the law of sin and death*]. **No one who is born of God** [*re-gene-rated*] **practices sin** [*lawlessness*], **because His seed** [*Agape: fuse-able DNA*] **abides in him**; and he cannot sin [*"the Agape of Christ controls us"*], because he is born of God [*DNA of Triune-Agape*]. By this the children of God and the children of the devil are obvious: anyone who does not **practice righteousness** [*reciprocal gene-rosity*] is not of God, nor the one who does not Agape [*sacrificially share himself with*] his brother (1 John 3:4-10).

As re-gene-rating "children of God," even now we are heirs of "the perfect [*incorruptible*] law, the law of liberty [*freedom*]…the royal law [*lit. the law of our King*]" (James 1:23; 2:8). The seed of this new, self-sharing nature matures within each of us by practice with one another. Since the law of Agape does not work by enforcement or coercion, we must willingly *yield* to this internal law: "put on **Agape** [*the fuse-able DNA of God in Christ*] which is **the perfect bond of unity** [*lit. the uniting bond of perfection*]" (Col. 3:14). By practice, you and I are progressively acculturated together into the cohabitation of our Triune-God. John mapped out this journey of acculturation:

> Whoever confesses that Jesus is the Son of God [*Triune-Agape incarnate*], God abides in him, and he in God [*the Trinity and man cohabit in fusion in the God-Man Nucleus*]. We have come to know and have believed the love [*lit. Agape*] which God has for us [*Triune-Agape 'focused' upon us in Christ*]. **God is Agape** [*three sacrificial Self-sharers*], **and the one who abides in Agape** [*sacrificial self-sharing Love*] **abides in God, and God abides in him** [*mutual indwelling: the cohabitation of the kingdom*]. By this, **Agape is perfected** [*lit. telios: matured*] **with us** [*e.g. learning to lawfully cohabit together in coequality as Trinity-like self-sharers*], so that we may have **confidence in the day of judgment** [*God's verdict: is this individual a gene-rous sharer or de-gene-rate taker?*]; because as He is [*the Triune-God in Christ*], so also are we in this world [*Christ's many-membered body*].

There is no fear in Agape [*no instinct of self-preservation*]; but **perfect** [*lit. telios; mature*] **Agape casts out fear**, because fear involves **punishment**, and the one who fears [*personal loss, penalty*] is not **perfected in Agape** [*sacrificial self-sharing from an inward nature*]. We love [*lit. Agape*], because He [*God in Christ*] first loved us. If someone says, "I love [*lit. Agape*] God," and **hates his brother**, he is a liar [*lawless son of "Beliar": Worthless*]; for the one who does not **Agape** [*sacrificially share himself with*] **his brother** whom he has seen, cannot *Agape* [*sacrificially share himself with*] God whom he has not seen. And this **commandment** we have from Him [*the "Us" of our genesis*], that the one who loves [*lit. Agape*] God should love [*lit. Agape*] his brother also (1 John 4:15-21).

I consider the following verse to be one of the most fascinating and significant in the entire Bible: "**O Lord…Your statutes are my songs in the house of my pilgrimage**" (Ps. 119:54). Consider this paradox: how can a man make a pilgrim's journey *inside* a house? Further, who would pull off the bookshelf a volume entitled '*Statutory Law*' and eagerly devour it like a book of love-poetry? What kind of laws, statutes, and ordinances would penetrate and grip a man's heart-affections so deeply that they would emerge in his spontaneous singing like a bubbling spring?

Father, Son, and Spirit, Who dwell in fusion within the Nucleus/corpus of Christ, are *Themselves* a "house"—a cohabitation. When the psalmist refers to "Your statutes" he means the laws of coequality, reciprocal gene-rosity, and sacrificial Self-sharing— applications of the law of Agape—by which Father, Son, and Spirit *Themselves* abide together in the God-Man Jesus. It is this very same "**house**" and these very same "**statutes**" that the Trinity purpose to share with us.

As believers, you and I have already been "**adopted**" (Eph. 1:5)—bought out of the false-father's custody in "the domain of darkness" (Col. 1:13) and brought home into the cohabitation of the true Father. We are now being **acculturated** in the laws (ways) of this household of Self-sharers, which are still new, foreign, and strange to us. As adopted children, we have not yet learned how to abide, function, and flourish as coequals in "Father's house." Like Abraham, we are called to **emigrate** out of our acculturation in Worthless' world (our former life) and deeper into the kingdom of our Triune-God; you and I are journeying *within* "God is a dwelling place" (Deut. 33:27).

Though we are already living in this relational, inter-Personal cohabitation of God in Christ, it is such an extensive, shared estate that a "pilgrimage" *within* that house is required to enter, discover, and participate in all of its infinite fullnesses. Kingdom emigrants proceed together on this journey into the relational fullnesses *within* this "house" by observing, practicing, and **cherishing** (i.e. singing about) **the "statutes" of Agape**: reciprocal sacrificial self-sharing, coequality, and justice. Emigrating "in the house of my pilgrimage" means I am practicing and maturing as a sacrificial self-sharer together with you, my brothers and sisters, in the laws and ways of the cohabitation of our Triune-God. T. Austin Sparks explained:

> It was a company [*of diverse individuals*] on the day of Pentecost that received the **breath from heaven** [*Triune-Pnuema*].... The new creation is a company, it is **a Body** [*many-membered corpus*] **indwelt** by the Holy Spirit, **actuated** by the Holy Spirit, actually **made one** by the Holy Spirit. "*In one Spirit were we all baptized* [*fused*] *into one body*" (1 Cor. 12:13). The oneness is **the** [*fusion*] **oneness of the Holy Spirit**. "*Giving diligence to keep the unity of the Spirit*" (Eph. 4:3), not to *make* it but to *keep* it.

> A new creation...see what new creation Life means...**the proper regulated order of heavenly Life** [*the law and justice of three coequal Self-sharers*]. Heavenly Life is according to **heavenly law** [*Agape*]. It is **not lawless** [*eros*]. Each member of this body is not a law unto himself or herself. **We are bound** [*fused as coequals*] **by this integrating, regulating law**; that we are not allowed to be

independent. Here the Holy Spirit forbids it. We are not allowed to take the law into our own hands. We are **not allowed to act as individuals**; the Holy Spirit will not allow it.

There is a regulating order with this Life…. This Life expresses itself according to its own laws, as life does in every part of the organic creation. It follows its own lines… and you have **not to organize or systematize this…. The thing** [*fusion oneness*] **happens if the Life has its way** [*e.g. "do not quench the Spirit"*]….It will come about if the Holy Spirit is really having His way in terms of Life. **We** [*individual believers*] **are all in school** [*i.e. a fusion laboratory*] (T. Austin Sparks, *The Testimony of the Christ*, chap. 7).

3. Perverting Justice

Due to *eros* **rationale** (one-dimensional, 'me'-centered thinking) the vast majority of human beings imagine God to be a solitary Being rather than "Holy, Holy, Holy" (Isa. 6:8; Rev. 4:8)—three coequal Individuals: an "Us" in fusion Oneness. Enslaved in self-conscious individualism, it is natural and 'logical' for me to think of God as a projection of my own autonomous self. This monotheistic misconception of God leads to **monarchialism**: the idea that God is a solitary monarch, a king who is '**Possessor**' of His

own possessions. God is indeed a king—**"king of righteousness** [*Agape: three sacrificial Self-sharers fused as one God in reciprocal gene-rosity*]...**king of peace** [*three Eternals in relational harmony: fusion oneness*]" (Heb. 7:2). In Agape rationale (multi-dimensional, 'us'-centered thinking), we see and *know* this eternal King:

> **Righteousness** [*sacrificial Self-sharing*] and **justice** [*coequality*] are **the foundation of Your throne** [*three eros-free Self-sharers = one, incorruptible Triune-God*]; **lovingkindness** and **truth** [*the Light of gen-uine, relational fusion*] go before You (Ps. 89:14).

Man's faulty, monotheistic 'construct' of God seriously distorts and perverts our understanding of justice. Not only do we envision a solitary King, but an aloof Judge who can only render judicial verdicts out of self-interest no matter how 'noble' those decisions may seem to be. Further, countless millions have unwittingly adopted the absurd idea that Jesus, the merciful Son, stands as Advocate and Victim between us and His angry, judgmental Father; however, Jesus already exposed this misconception: **"For not even the Father judges anyone,** but He has given all judgment to the Son.... I did not come to judge the world, but to save the world" (John 5:22; 12:47).

Through the ages, believers have simply ignored

these words of Jesus that clearly reveal that the intent of the Triune-God toward mankind is not judgment but reconciliation. This 'factor' is essential to an accurate theological equation or proof, yet it has been omitted by the vast majority of theologians through history. Richard Rohr describes how this misconception of God has been perpetuated:

> The common Christian reading of the Bible is that Jesus "died for our sins"—either to pay a debt to the devil...or to pay a debt to God the Father. My hero, Franciscan philosopher and theologian John Duns Scotus (1266-1308)... was not guided by the Temple language of debt, atonement, or blood sacrifice.... He was inspired by the high level cosmic hymns in the first chapters of Colossians and Ephesians and the first chapter of John's Gospel.
>
> Christians have paid a huge price for what theologians called "substitutionary atonement theory"—the strange idea that before God could love us God needed and demanded Jesus to be a blood sacrifice to atone for our sin-drenched humanity. With that view, salvation depends upon a problem instead of a divine proclamation about the core nature of reality [Triune-Agape]. As if God could need payment, and even a very violent transaction, to be able to love and accept "his" own children—a message that those with an angry,

distant, absent, or abusive father were already far too programmed to believe.

For Scotus, the incarnation of God and the redemption of the world could never be a mere mop-up exercise in response [reaction] to human sinfulness, but the **proactive** work of God from the very beginning. We were "chosen in Christ before the world was made" (Eph. 1:4). Our sin could not possibly be the motive for the divine incarnation, but only perfect love and divine self-revelation! For Scotus, God never merely **reacts**, but always supremely and freely **acts**, and always acts totally out of love [superabundant Triune-Agape]. Scotus was very **Trinitarian**.

The best way I can summarize how Scotus tried to change the old notion of **retributive justice** is this: Jesus did not come to change the mind of God about humanity (it did not need changing)! Jesus came to change the mind of humanity about God. God in Jesus moved people beyond the counting, weighing, and **punishing model**, that the ego prefers, to the utterly new world that Jesus offered, where God's abundance has made any **economy of merit**, sacrifice, reparation, or atonement both unhelpful and unnecessary. Jesus undid "once and for all" (Hebrews 7:27; 9:12; 10:10) all notions of human and animal sacrifice and replaced them with his new **economy of grace**, which is the very heart of the gospel revolution.

Jesus was meant to be a game changer for the human psyche and for religion itself. When we begin negatively, or focused on the problem, **we never get out of the hamster wheel** [perpetual legalism]. To this day we begin with and continue to focus on sin, when the crucified one was pointing us toward a **primal solidarity** [e.g. coequals in relational fusion] with the very suffering of God and all of creation. This changes everything. Change the starting point, change the trajectory! We all need to know that *God does not love us because we are good; God loves us because God is good.* (Richard Rohr, *Love, Not Atonement*; adapted from *Eager to Love: The Alternative Way of Francis of Assisi*, pp. 183-188).

Building upon Scotus' assessment of how God's nature and intent toward mankind has been grievously misrepresented and corrupted through the ages, C. Baxter Kruger provides a brilliant, historical understanding of the disastrous consequences of this misconception—the "legalization of God":

Foreign ideas about God, ideas which have not been brought before the bar of the

Trinity and converted, ideas that may seem obvious and quite plausible to the natural mind, have been allowed to exist side by side with the revelation of God in Christ. These unconverted ideas have not only distorted our understanding of God; they have also shaped our understanding of God's relationship with humanity—with disastrous results.... The holiness of God, the sovereignty and righteousness and justice of God, the love and wrath of God are all essentially Trinitarian concepts.... Properly understood, the holiness of God is a Trinitarian idea. If we took the joy and the fullness and the love of the Father, Son, and Spirit, their mutual delight and passion, the sheer togetherness of their relationship, its intimacy, harmony, and wholeness, and rolled them all into one word, it would be "holiness."

...In the Western tradition, however, the Christian conversion of the idea of holiness, its Trinitarianization, never really developed. Instead, the holiness of God was detached from the Trinity and reconceived within the world of Roman jurisprudence. It was revisioned through Roman concepts of law and order, crime and punishment, blind and cold justice. Reconceived within this stainless steel world of pure law, "holiness" came to mean "legal perfection" or "moral rectitude"…. We allowed the holiness of God to be legalized. The face of God was tarred with the legal brush, so tarred that the fellowship of the Father, Son, and Spirit, was virtually eclipsed…It became "natural" to think legally, to frame the question of God's relationship to man in terms of law and guilt and punishment….

The eternal purpose of this Triune God is not to place us under law and turn us into religious legalists, but to include us in their relationship…. If we must speak in terms of law, then we must say that the law of this universe is the primal decision of the Father, Son, and Spirit to **give humanity a place in the Trinitarian life**…. But here, in the legal model…Jesus has come to save us not from ourselves and the catastrophe of Adam, but from God. Changing God has become the object of Christ's work….

When we give the Trinity its proper place in our thinking, however, we see clearly that God is eternally "for us." Before the foundation of the world, the Father, Son and Spirit set their determined love upon us and set their hand to the plow to bring us into the circle of their shared life…. Punishment has never been the point….The legal model forces us to think of

God as divided (C. Baxter Kruger, *Jesus and the Undoing of Adam*, p. 42-46, Perichoresis Press, 2001).

See how *de-gene-rate* human beings misinterpret "Justice" as heartless, detached retribution from an aloof, unknowable Source:

When Paul had gathered a bundle of sticks and laid them on the fire, a **viper** came out because of the heat and fastened itself on his hand. When the natives saw the creature hanging from his hand, they began saying to one another, "**Undoubtedly this man is a murderer**, and though he has been saved from the sea [*shipwreck*], **Justice has not allowed him to live**." However, he shook the creature off into the fire and suffered no harm (Acts 28:3-5).

This approach to justice as heartless retribution causes us to *rejoice* when calamity falls upon another person or nation, for example: a natural disaster is "Justice" targeting a specific people group whom we consider evil; economic collapse is "Justice" repaying those who have defrauded us; A.I.D.S. is "Justice" eliminating sexual deviants; etc. Due to our distorted and inadequate knowledge of the "true" Triune-God, our interpretation of justice is warped, our legal systems are perverted, and our judgments, verdicts, retributions, and rewards are twisted:

> Millions of human beings have been slaughtered and **constrained to slaughter each other** by being more or less persuaded that their deaths would be **serving Justice and Law.** By His readiness to become the **victim** of such belief, Jesus unmasked this monstrous falsity... (Jean Lasserre, *War and the Gospel*).

Consider how the misconception of God as a solitary, Self-exalting Monarch and a capricious, Self-serving Judge has influenced and shaped human history—the inhumane way men and women have treated one another! Largely through misguided religion, "the father of the lie" has grossly misrepresented God to instigate and perpetuate relational fission, oppression, war, and destruction on the earth. The prophet Habakkuk observed:

> Strife exists and contention arises [*relational fission*], therefore **the law** [*Agape: sacrificial self-sharing*] **is ignored** [*lit. numbed*] **and justice** [*coequality of individuals*] **is never upheld.** For the wicked surround the righteous; therefore **justice comes out perverted...** They are dreaded and feared; **their justice and authority originate with** [*lit. proceed from*] **themselves** [*e.g. their de-gene-rate, eros nature: "the lie"*]. Their horses are swifter than

leopards and keener than wolves [*predatory opportunists*] in the evening (Hab. 1:3-8).

Before the time of the kings of Israel, God led and governed the nation through a series of "judges" who were sovereignly raised up and guided by the Spirit. From a small boy, God mentored the prophet Samuel as a faithful, incorruptible steward-son, yet the people of Israel said to him, "**Give us a king to judge us**" (1 Sam. 8:6).

The Lord said to Samuel, "Listen to the voice of the people…for they have not rejected you, but **they have rejected Me** [*three incorruptible Self-sharers*] **from being king over them**… however, you shall solemnly **warn** them…". Samuel said to the people, "This will be the procedure of the king who will reign over you: **he will take your sons** and place them *for* **himself** in his chariots.…He will appoint *for* himself commanders…and some to do his plowing and to reap his harvest and to make his weapons of war. **He will also take your daughters** *for* perfumers and cooks and bakers. He will take the best…He will take… He will also take…He will take…and **you yourselves will become his servants**.

Then you will cry out in that day because of your king [*a de-gene-rate individualist, corrupt opportunist: an unjust judge*] whom **you have chosen for yourselves**, but the Lord will not answer you in that day." Nevertheless, the people refused to listen to the voice of Samuel, and they said, "No, but there shall be a king over us, that we also may be like all the nations, **that our king may judge us**…" (1 Sam. 8:7-20).

For many years, David suffered gross injustice at the hands of Saul, the first king who judged Israel. As the next anointed king, David was also compelled by his own corrupt nature to make several mega-mistakes. In repentant confession, David acknowledged to the Lord, "You [*the incorruptible Triune-God*] are **justified** when You speak and **blameless** when You judge" (Ps. 51:4). Due to our faulty, monotheistic construct of God, the Spirit must intervene and "**unveil**" these three sacrificial Self-sharers for us through the Scriptures. None of the Individuals of the Trinity act as a Proprietor; rather, each is a Steward of One Another and of the Oneness They share. Each is a *gene-rous* Steward of Their creation *for* One Another and *for* us.

Those who are eclipsed from the giving and forgiving Triune-God of *Agape* have no recourse but to attempt self-forgiveness and self-justification. Dietrich Bonhoeffer described this futile exercise as "**granting ourselves absolution**." Bonhoeffer explained, "Self-forgiveness can never lead to a breach with sin [*e.g. deliverance from our eros nature, rationale, and behavior*]; this can only be accomplished by **the judging and pardoning Word of God itself**" (*Life Together*, p. 116). God's judgments are not an end in themselves; the Word of God judges us to make possible our redemption, repentance, pardon, cleansing, re-gene-ration, and restoration.

Those who come, by faith, to see and know the Triune-Redeemer gain a radically different perspective on justice; they clearly distinguish God's justice from capricious anger, Self-interest, or retribution. Jeremiah prayed, "**Correct me** [*the wayward individualist*], **O Lord**, **but with justice** [*discipline in self-sharing coequality*]; **not with Your anger**, or You will bring me to nothing" (Jer. 10:24). David, conscious of his need for daily correction, prayed, "**Let my judgment come forth from Your Presence** [*Holy, Holy, Holy: three coequal Self-sharers in fusion*]; let Your eyes look with **equity**. You have tried my heart…" (Ps. 17:2-3). For us who are emigrating into the kingdom, Triune-justice is not something to fear, but our dearest friend and ally in a war against "the law of sin and death," which persists and often prevails within us:

> The exercise of justice [*restoring freedom and coequality among individuals*] is **joy** for the righteous [*sacrificial self-sharers*], but **terror** to the workers of iniquity (Prov. 21:15).

4. The "severity of God"

Paul urged, "Behold then **the kindness and severity of God...**" (Rom. 11:22). The Scriptures repeatedly illustrate how our Triune-God becomes angry yet "is slow to anger" (Ex. 34:6) and how the actions and measures of the "God of justice" can be very severe. David wrote another related *God is* statement: "**God is a righteous Judge** [*three incorruptible Self-sharers*] **and a God who has indignation every day** [*angry abhorrence over man's corruption, self-worth-ship, and injustice to one another*]" (Ps. 7:11). David added, "Do homage to the Son that He not become angry, and you perish in the way, for **His wrath may soon be kindled**. How blessed are all who take refuge in Him [*fuse into the Nucleus of the Triune-God*]!" (Ps. 2:12).

We believers often fail to recognize that God's kindness *and* God's severity are *both* **interventions motivated by pure Agape**—redemptive measures to bring willful individualists to repentance. Through the Scriptures, let's establish in our thinking some parameters on the true purpose of justice and precisely why God executes severe judgment. Accurately understanding "the Lord is a God of justice" is essential and urgent because our misconception of God is precisely the thing that compels us to criticize, accuse, indict, and **pass judgment on one another** in a way that precipitates relational fission and keeps us eclipsed from the kingdom! James wrote:

So speak and so act as those who are to be judged by **the law of liberty** [*e.g. if I am free from self-worth-ship, I am free to be a sacrificial self-sharer*]. For judgment will be merciless to one who has shown no mercy; **mercy triumphs over judgment** (James 2:12-13).

Jeremiah witnessed the brutal, predatory nation of Babylon drag off his own people of Judah into exile according to God's sentence of judgment, yet in his book of Lamentations, this "weeping prophet" revealed God's true, unseen motive:

For the Lord will not reject forever, for if He causes grief, then He will have compassion according to His abundant lovingkindness [*"mercy triumphs over judgment"*]. For **He does not afflict willingly, or grieve the sons of men** [*e.g. capriciously*]. To crush under His feet all the prisoners of the land [*retribution to those already condemned*], to **deprive a man of justice** [*lit. turn aside a man in his case; marginalize an individual*] in the presence of the Most High, to **defraud** [*lit. make crooked*] a man in his lawsuit—of these things the Lord does not approve (Lam. 3:31-38).

The foremost reason God deals severely with you and me is that we callously and capriciously withhold mercy from one another *after* we have received God's unfathomable and unmerited mercy. Meditate on the conclusion of Jesus' parable of the two debtors:

> Summoning him, his lord said to him, "You wicked slave, I forgave you all that debt because you pleaded with me. Should you not also have had **mercy on your fellow slave**, in the same way that I had mercy on you?" And his lord, **moved with anger**, handed him over to the torturers until he should repay all that was owed him. My heavenly Father will also do the same to you [*as a redemptive, disciplinary measure*], if each of you does not forgive his brother from your heart (Matt. 18:32-35).

God spoke through the prophet Amos, "I will not revoke Edom's punishment because he pursued his brother with the sword while he **stifled** [*lit. corrupted*] **his compassion**; his anger also tore continually" (Amos 1:11). God's judgments are not an end in themselves but initiatives of His mercy to save each individual from individualism and **disciplinary measures of His redemptive justice to teach selfish men how to share!** It is the willful obstinacy of "stiff-necked" human beings, who consume themselves and others around them in self-worth-ship, that makes God's severity necessary. There is *not* a dark, secret desire within the Triune-God that needs to execute retribution for Self-gratification, wants to retaliate for His own amusement, or delights in anyone's downfall.

Paul testified:

> I was formerly a blasphemer and a persecutor and a violent aggressor [*a religious opportunist*]. Yet I was shown mercy because I **acted ignorantly in unbelief** [*eclipsed from the justice of Triune-Agape*]; and the grace of our Lord was more than abundant, with the faith and Agape which are found in Christ Jesus. He came into the world to **save sinners** [*eros individualists*], among whom I am foremost of all. Yet for this reason I found mercy, so that in me as the foremost, **Jesus Christ might demonstrate His perfect patience** as an example for those [*like you and me*] who would believe in Him for eternal life (1 Tim. 1:13-16).

In the final volume of *God Magnified*, we will study "the Lord, whose name is Jealous, is a jealous God" (Ex. 34:14) and "the Lord your God is a consuming fire, a jealous God" (Dt. 4:24; Heb. 12:29). As individualists tyrannized by eros, you and I are **jealous-*of*** one another; in Agape Father, Son, and Spirit are **jealous-*for*** One Another and *for* us. The consuming fire of "**godly** [*Trinity-like*] **jealousy**" (2 Cor. 11:2) is God's core motivation for severe judgment. God is *jealous-for* His glory to be revealed in every human being, even "the foremost" of sinners like Saul the Pharisee. It is not the individual sinner that God hates but the de-gene-rate, eros nature of self-worth-ship that tyrannizes that individual. In *jealousy-for* us, the Triune-God of Agape will use whatever measures of severity that are necessary to eradicate "the law of sin and death" at work within us. Further, God is particularly *jealous-for* believers who willingly suffer persecution for His sake. Paul wrote:

> We ourselves speak proudly of you…for your perseverance and faith in the midst of all your persecutions and afflictions which you endure. This is **a plain indication of God's righteous judgment** so that you will be considered worthy of the kingdom of God [*fit to cohabit with other sacrificial self-sharers in coequality*], for which indeed you are suffering [*e.g. being tested, proven, and matured in Agape*]. For after all it is only **just** for God [*Three jealous-for One Another and for you*] to **repay with affliction** those who afflict you, and to give relief to you who are afflicted… (2 Thess. 1:4-7).

Motivated by *jealousy-for* One Another and *for* you, Father, Son, and Spirit repay those who injure you; therefore, it is unnecessary, even counterproductive, to "take your own revenge" (Rom. 12:19). God's repayment is not the unrestrained vengeance of **retribution** as it is defined according to corrupt, eros rationale, motivated by jealousy-of (envy). God spoke to Ezekiel, "Say to them, '**As I live!**' declares the Lord

God, '**I take no pleasure in the death of the wicked**, **but rather that the wicked** [*the individualist*] **turn from his way** [*e.g. opportunism in self-worth-ship*] **and live** [*in relational coequality*]'" (Ezek. 33:11).

For instance, God could have delivered the enslaved people of Israel out of Egypt in one day; the purpose of sending the series of plagues upon Egypt had more to do with demonstrating Gods' *jealousy-for* Israel and proving to a degraded, slave-minded people their precious value to Him, not merely taking opportunity to annihilate their captors. Though earthly governments are inadequate and corrupt, Paul recognized them as instruments of God's *jealousy-for*:

> But if you do what is evil [*lawlessness: eros opportunism*] be afraid; for **governing authority** does not bear the sword for nothing; for it is a **minister of God** [*three Self-sharers*], an **avenger** who brings wrath on the one who practices evil [*preying on others for self-indulgence*] (Rom. 13:1-4).

Sacrificial Son-giving Love, is the most compelling evidence that the "severity of God" is purely motivated by Agape. Dwelling in the Nucleus of Christ, the Triune-God bore in Himself all of the judgments He executed upon man from Eden and throughout the history of mankind. A careful study of Jesus' agony, betrayal, arrest, interrogation, torture, and crucifixion reveal that these events were sovereignly choreographed by the Triune-God for the purpose of comprehensively absorbing into Himself all the curses, judgments, verdicts, wrath, and repayments ever decreed against de-gene-rate mankind or that corrupt human beings simply reaped from what they had sowed. For further study, read Lifechangers *Plumbline* entitled *Thorn-crowned Son of Man*.

In Christ, the Triune-God not only sacrificially bore man's due punishment, Father, Son, and Spirit also comprehensively exhausted into the human Nucleus of Their Oneness the full power of our relational fission as "children of darkness." This **extreme Self-forsaking Love** is certainly not the act of a solitary Judge whose fundamental motivation is **capricious retribution**. In all of these seemingly contradictory measures—judging and then sacrificially bearing the consequences of His own judgments—**God is working toward something**, building an unshakable kingdom of *gen-uine* coequality, a cohabitation of free, self-emptied, self-sharing individuals fused into one unshakable God-Man Nucleus! "Behold, I AM making all things new" (Rev. 21:5).

5. Self-exaltation and Injustice

An individualist inebriated by self-worth-ship cannot be taught true justice. "**God** [*three sacrificial Self-sharers*] **leads the humble** [*self-emptied*] **in justice** [*relational coequality*], and **He teaches the humble** [*self-emptied*] **His way** [*reciprocal gene-rosity*]" (Ps.

25:9). Injustice, or lawlessness, is the inevitable consequence of **self-worth-ship** and "**self-exaltation**" (Jer. 48:29). If I consider *your* worth to be inferior to *my own*, it follows that I deserve to have whatever I am able to exact from you by defrauding, exploiting, and oppressing you; this is the rationale of a self-deceived deceiver who has matured in "the lie." American colloquialisms often reveal this subterranean motive: "What can I do *for* you?" is often phrased "What can I *do* you *for*?"

Justice is God's means of **interrupting** individualists on their path of 'upward descent': **confronting** self-worth-ship and self-exaltation; **exposing** lawlessness, opportunism, and oppression; and **preserving** the freedom and coequality of individuals according to the law of Agape: "God is the Judge [*Equalizer*]; He puts down one and exalts another" (Ps. 75:7). Due to the merciful interventions of God's justice, it is said, "Every con has an expiration date."

> On an appointed day Herod [*King of Israel*], having put on his royal apparel, took his seat on the rostrum and began delivering an address to them. The people kept crying out, "The voice of a god and not of a man!" And immediately an angel of the Lord struck him because he did not give God the glory, and he was eaten by worms and died (Acts 12:21-23).

The Lord sent angels to rescue Lot from Sodom saying, "bring them [*your relatives*] out of the place; for we are about to destroy this place, because their outcry [*e.g. self-exaltation in self-worth-ship*] has become so great before the Lord that the Lord has sent us to destroy it" (Gen. 19:12-13). According to the law of upward descent, when Worthless' nature of self-exaltation has come to full maturity in an individual or in a people, moving them to indulge self at the expense of others, justice intervenes in whatever measure of severity is necessary to interrupt the momentum of corruption and contain and cleanse the spreading infection.

God said to Abram, "Know for certain that your descendants…will be enslaved and oppressed four hundred years. But I will also judge the nation [*Egypt*] whom they will serve, and afterward they will come out with many possessions…they will return here [*promised land of Canaan*], for **the iniquity of the Amorite** [*occupants whom I will "dispossess"*] **is not yet complete** [*e.g. they have not yet come to full maturity in Worthless' nature*]" (Gen. 15:13-16).

Blinded by self-focus, and inebriated by self-worth-ship, we are too short-sighted to see the inevitable, counter-productive outcome of willfully choosing the way of upward descent. Self-exaltation is our default-mode, but where does it come from? Solomon observed, "If you see oppression of the poor and **denial of justice** [*coequality*] **and righteousness** [*reciprocal self-sharing; gene-rosity*] in the province, do not be shocked at the sight; for one official watches over another official, and there are **higher officials over them** [*e.g. the socio-economic pyramid of Worthless' world*]" (Eccl. 5:8). Self-exaltation, lawless opportunism, and injustice all have their origin in Worthless, "the father of lies [*lit. the lie*]" (John 8:44). The *de-gene-rate* nature of this false-father is in each of us, yet in some, like King Herod, Absalom, Nebuchadnezzar, and even Jonah, it matures to such a degree that requires Triune-Justice to intervene with severity. Paul identified the source of lawlessness at work in man:

With regard to the coming [*return*] of our Lord Jesus Christ and our gathering together to Him [*perfected together in fusion in the God-Man Nucleus*]…the **apostasy** [*falling away*] comes first, and **the man of lawlessness** is revealed, the son of destruction [*agent of fission*], who opposes and **exalts himself** above every so-called god or object of worship [*self-worth-ship*], so that he takes his seat [*as a lawless, corrupt judge*] in the temple of God, displaying himself as being God [*e.g. the way of upward descent*]….For **the mystery of lawlessness** [*fission power*] is already at work….

That **lawless one** will be revealed whom the Lord will slay with the breath of His mouth [*Triune-Pneuma*] and bring to an end by the appearance of His coming [*unshielded Light of the fusion of God in Christ*]; that is the one whose coming is in accord with **the activity of Satan** [*the fallen usurper*] (2 Thess. 2:1-12).

One expects to find injustice around every corner in the secular world, but it is far more appalling and grievous to discover just how common injustice is among God's people: "For I, the Lord [*three Self-sharers*], **love justice, I hate robbery with iniquity in the burnt offering** [*hypocrisy, religious opportunism*]" (Isa. 61:8). We believers do not merely withhold justice from one another, but also from God! Religious injustice is Agape with hypocrisy—the pretense of sharing "all" or giving the first and best to God as He deserves, yet beneath lies **calculated 'withholding'** motivated by self-worth-ship and self-exaltation—"I deserve to have."

Cain was first to give an offering with pretense to God, while Abel genuinely shared (Gen. 4:5). Ananias and Sapphira's unjust offering was interrupted by the severity of God (Acts 5:1-11). Jesus said, "But woe to you Pharisees! For you pay tithe of mint and rue and cumin [*self-righteous, self-promoting legalism*], and yet **disregard justice and the Agape of God** [*self-sharing coequality*]" (Luke 11:42). If we cannot sacrificially share with God, how can we share with one another, and vice versa? Paul admonished the Corinthian believers:

Does any one of you, when he has a case against his neighbor, **dare to go to law before the unrighteous** and not before the saints? Or do you not know that **the saints** [*lit. holy ones; sacrificial self-sharers*] **will judge the world**? If the world is judged by you, are you not competent [*e.g. mature enough*] to constitute the smallest law courts? Do you not know that we will judge angels? How much more matters of this life? So if you have law courts dealing with matters of this life, do you appoint them [*de-gene-rate sons of Worthless*] as **judges** who are of no account in the church [*e.g. not incorporated into Christ's corpus*]? I say this to your shame.

Is it so, that there is not among you one wise man [*mature self-sharer practiced in Agape rationale*] who will be able to decide between his brethren, but **brother goes to law with brother**, and that before unbelievers? Actually, then, **it is already a defeat for you** [*forfeiture to Worthless*], **that you have lawsuits with one another** [*escalated counter-reactions, relational fission*]. Why not rather be wronged? **Why not rather be defrauded** [*bear the loss individually for the sake of the whole body*]? On the contrary, you yourselves wrong and defraud [*practice religious opportunism*]. You do this even to your brethren (1 Cor. 6:1-8).

Ideally, civil and criminal courts of law are established in nations and local communities to uphold justice—to preserve freedom and equality among all the individual human beings who cohabit together. In these courts, a prosecutor represents the **plaintiff** (victim), a defense attorney represents the **accused** (violator), and a **judge** presides over them. Motivated by the hope of monetary compensation (self-indulgence), the payoff of retribution (i.e. 'I will have my revenge'), or vindication of one's own reputation (self-preservation in self-worth-ship), both the plaintiff and the accused **strategize to win the case** unaware they are on the same path of **upward descent**. On the courthouse steps, the victor addresses the news reporters, saying, "Justice has prevailed!" In private with his lawyer, he boasts, "We tipped the scales of justice on my side." However, if he had "ears to hear," the Triune-God would say to him, "it is already a defeat for you"—you gained a worthless settlement at the cost of losing your precious brother.

Justice, which is the functional expression of the law of Agape written into the very DNA of Father, Son, and Spirit, simply ensures that each Individual receives "all things" that the other Two deem Him *worthy* to receive and whole-heartedly award to Him by Self-sacrifice. None of the Three needs to contend for His own 'rights' because the other Two uphold and exalt Him in *jealous-for* Love. Isaiah prophesied how the transcendent reality of Triune-Justice would be revealed to us in the God-Man Jesus:

> Each of us [*individualists*] has turned to his own way [*self-will, fission*]; but **the Lord has caused the iniquity** [*corruption, injustice*] **of us all to fall on Him** [*on Himself: Jesus, the Nucleus of the Trinity*]. He was oppressed and He was afflicted, yet He did not open His mouth [*in Self-defense*]; like a **lamb** that is led to slaughter, and like a sheep that is silent before its shearers [*accusers*], so He did not open His mouth [*in Self-justification*]. By oppression and **judgment** [*injustice*] He was taken away (Isa. 53:6-8).

In varying degrees of skill and maturity, earthly judges are corrupt because every judge is a de-generate human being in whom "the law of sin and death" is ruling. In the case of a judge who is also a believer, lawlessness may not be prevailing, yet it is still resident and at work within him. Therefore, apart from God's instruction to a judge and his ability to hear and yield to God's just decisions, **a judge cannot avoid deciding a case in his own self-interest**: in the interest of his own personal bias, or in the interest of the party who is most likely to give him a payoff, or in the interest of his public image and election or reappointment.

Solomon observed, "**The king gives stability** [*relational solidarity, peace*] **to the land by justice** [*preserving freedom and coequality as God's sacrificial self-sharing steward*], **but a man who takes a bribe** [*reciprocal eros payoff at others' expense*] **overthrows it** [*e.g. hands over to Worthless the 'Deed and Trust' of the cohabitation*]" (Prov. 29:4). Pontius Pilate knew for certain that Jesus was innocent, and "he knew that the chief priests had handed Jesus over because of envy" (Matt. 15:10); however, in the interests of his own public image and future political career as a Roman governor, Pilate was forced to condemn Jesus to be scourged and crucified. Like Pilate, though I may be reluctant to judge another who is falsely accused, when it's a question of choosing him or me, it's *me* by default. Injustice not only transpires in courtrooms, but in families, workplaces, and even Christian communities.

As King David's son, Solomon witnessed how even the most sincere men of God were *compelled* by their corrupt nature to abuse the power of judgment. When Solomon succeeded David as king, he humbly acknowledged that he was simply *not* qualified to judge:

The Lord appeared to Solomon in a dream... ."Ask what you wish Me to give you." Then Solomon said, "...You have made Your servant king in place of my father David, yet I am but a little child; I do not know how to go out or come in. Your servant is in the midst of Your people which You have chosen, a great people which are too many to be numbered or counted. So **give Your servant an understanding heart** [*lit. a hearing heart; dynamic God-conscious dependence*] **to judge Your people to discern between good and evil** [*Agape and eros*]. For who is able to judge this great people of Yours?"

It was **pleasing** in the sight of the Lord that Solomon had asked this thing [*to "seek first His" as a steward*].... "Because you have asked this thing and have not asked **for yourself long life** [*self-preservation*], nor have you asked **riches for yourself** [*self-gratification*], nor have you asked **for the life of your enemies** [*revenge, self-exaltation*], but have asked for yourself **discernment** [*lit. hearing*] **to understand justice** [*freedom and coequality for My people*], behold, I have done according to your words....I have given you a wise and discerning heart....I have also given you what you have not asked, both riches and honor..." (1 Kings 3:5-14).

6. Pawns of "the Accuser"

Suppose a confidential survey is taken among individual believers (including workers, pastors, missionaries, etc.) to determine what, in their opinion, is the main source of strife, enmity, injury, and relational fission that plague and weaken their Christian communities. I venture to guess that **speaking against one another** in criticism, accusation, malicious gossip, and judgment would certainly top the list of responses. Jesus said, "Do not judge so that you will not be judged. For in the way you **judge**, you will be **judged**; and by your standard of measure, it will be measured to you" (Matt. 7:1-2). If each of us has repeatedly suffered as a victim of accusations and capricious judgments, why is it that we cannot stop inflicting it on one another? Curiously, we all know "God is the Judge" (Ps. 75:7), but Jesus made clear that **even God does not judge!**

> God did not send the Son into the world to judge the world, but that the world might be saved through Him.... For **not even the Father judges anyone**, but He has given all judgment to the Son.... "If anyone hears My sayings and does not keep them, **I do not judge him**; for I did not come to judge the world, but to save the world. He who rejects Me [*the Nucleus of the Trinity*] and does not receive My sayings, has one who judges him; **the word I spoke** [*e.g. revelation of Triune-Agape I embodied, taught, modeled, and demonstrated*] **is what will judge him at the last day**" (John 3:17; 5:22; 12:47-48).

The word "**accuser**" accurately describes a law-enforcement officer, prosecutor, witness, or judge who **speaks against** someone in an interrogation or a trial. The Greek word for "accuser" is *katēgoros* from which we get the term **categorize**. As a police officer handcuffs a suspect whom he has apprehended, he says, "You are under arrest for… (specific category of crime or violation)…anything you say can and will be **used against you** in a court of law…." In Revelation, John described the activity of Satan: "the **accuser** [*lit. categorizer*] of our brethren has been thrown down [*e.g. from self-exaltation*], he who **accuses** [*lit. categorizes*] them before God day and night" (Rev. 12:10).

C. Baxter Kruger observed, "modern evangelical theology translated God and God's relationship with human beings through the **meat-grinder of legal categories**" (*Jesus and the Undoing of Adam*, p. 45). Fault-finding, accusing, and judging another literally means I find a **category** to put him in—"he is a…" or "she always…" or "remember what he did last time…." Motivated by individualism, self-justification, and self-exaltation, I categorize another so I don't have to acknowledge and value their individuality, and I will not be required to sacrificially share with them or forgive and forebear them as my **coequal**. Further, categorizing another person **dehumanizes** that individual in my thinking and makes it easier to justify skirting the law in order to exploit them. James described one manifestation of the fission dynamic of categorizing:

Do not hold...an attitude of **personal favoritism**. For if a man comes into your assembly with a gold ring and dressed in fine clothes, and there also comes in a poor man in dirty clothes, and you pay special attention to the one who is wearing the fine clothes, and say, "You sit here in a good place," and you say to the poor man, "You stand over there, or sit down by my footstool," have you not **made distinctions among yourselves** [*categorizing men according to Worthless' hierarchical economy*], **and become judges with evil motives** [*eros opportunism*]?...You have dishonored [*devalued*] the poor man....If, however, you are **fulfilling the royal law** [*of our Triune-Creator*] according to the Scripture, "You shall love your neighbor as [*in place of*] yourself," you are doing well. But if you show **partiality**, you are committing sin and are convicted by the law [*of Agape: sacrificial self-sharing coequality*] as transgressors [*opportunists*] (James 2:1-9).

Worthless is a formidable "**accuser** [*categorizer*]" because he is an **expert legalist**. In endless attempts to gain ascendency over God, who is bound to human beings as His cherished inheritance, the false-father perverts and misappropriates God's law to exalt himself over us and hold us hostage. As a legal opportunist, Satan is a practiced '**ambulance chaser**' who covertly recruits us into his schemes to sow seeds of relational fission. Self-justification, self-exaltation, legalism, and a judgmental (categorizing) spirit are all manifestations of the unclean spirit of "the accuser" (the father of the lie) in human beings. God exposed the connection between "**the pointing of the finger** [*categorizing*] **and speaking wickedness**" (Isa. 58:9). Nit-picking, finger-pointing, back-biting, and mud-slinging are expressions of Worthless' nature persisting in us. Dietrich Bonhoeffer explained:

> From the first moment when a man meets another person he is **looking for a strategic position** he can assume and hold over against that person....Where is there a person who does not with instinctive sureness find the spot where he can stand and defend himself, but which he will never give up to another, for which he will fight with all the drive of his **instinct of self-assertion**? All this can occur in the most polite or even pious environment....
>
> **It is the struggle of the natural man for self-justification**. He finds it only in comparing himself with others, in condemning and judging others. **Self-justification and judging others** go together, as **justification by grace and serving others** go together (Dietrich Bonhoeffer, *Life Together*, p. 90).

The justice of God is always **proactive**; counterfeit justice is always **reactionary**. The Triune-God is "I AM who I AM" (Ex. 3:14). As a created, fallen being, Lucifer (aka. Satan) can only *react* in opposition to all that God is. God *acts* to implement justice; Worthless and his human agents *react*. Like the scribes and Pharisees, you and I have bought into the unclean spirit of "the accuser [*categorizer*]" and become **mindless automatons** who, with calloused indifference, treat others inhumanely while "just following orders." We might say, "I don't write the laws, I just enforce them." We are not *proactive* men led by the Spirit, but men who unwittingly lend all our strength to ill-conceived crusades under the **pretense of correcting injustice**, but in **reaction** we are precipitating a much greater crisis and broader injustice!

Jesus was determined to go to Jerusalem [*Man of action*]…and went and entered a village of the **Samaritans** [*mixed race considered unclean by Jews*]…but they **did not receive Him**, because He was traveling toward Jerusalem [*men of racial and political reaction*]. When **James and John** saw this [*reaction*], they said, "Lord, do You want us to **command fire to come down from heaven and consume them** [*e.g. counter-reaction*]?" But He [*the Equalizer*] turned and rebuked them, and said, "You do not know what **spirit** you are of [*e.g. the accuser: categorizer*]…" (Luke 9:51-56).

Blinded by self-focus, inebriated by self-worth-ship, and deluded by self-righteousness, we legalists are incapable of seeing the value (coequality) of the individuals around us. All we can see is **law and law-enforcement**—forcing others into rigid legal categories and feeling justified and gratified that we have "served" Justice. Observing and being mentored by other corrupt legalists, we come to believe we were somehow deputized by Jesus and received our 'sheriff's badge' from God. In fact, it is Worthless "the accuser [*categorizer*]" who, from concealment, recruited us and goads us to **react against others** to further his schemes of relational fission.

Jesus made clear that God is not a sheriff, and God "does not judge anyone;" why then would the Trinity deputize me to judge others? They have given me one solitary mandate—to receive and reciprocate Agape—engaging others as **coequals** with sacrificial compassion, mercy, forgiveness, forbearance, altruism. In an attempt to help us to see and participate in the kindom, Bob Mumford solemnly urged us, **"Turn in your sheriff's badge!"**

The deceptive snare of legalism, accusation, and judgment is buying into the carefully-crafted lie that I must defend God—**a God who does not defend Himself!** Yet, the real motivation has nothing to do with jealousy-*for* God, but rather jealousy-*of*. Motivated by self-justification and self-promotion, I defend the belief-system of the group or denomination into which I have been acculturated by forcing others into its legal categories. Paul recognized how easily immature believers manifest the unclean spirit of "the accuser [*categorizer*]" and are used as unwitting pawns of this false-father; therefore, he urged, "**let us not judge one another anymore**" (Rom. 14:13). James added:

> Humble yourselves in the presence of the Lord, and he will exalt you [*e.g. embrace 'downward ascent' as your new default mode*]. **Do not speak against one another**, brethren. He who speaks against his brother or judges [*exalts himself above*] his brother, speaks against the law and **judges the law** [*exalts himself above Triune-Agape*]; but if you judge the law, you are not a doer of the law but a [*lawless*] judge of it. **There is only one Lawgiver and Judge**, the One [*Triune-God*] who is able to save and to destroy; but who are you to judge your neighbor? (James 4:10-12).

God's servant **Job** "was blameless, upright, fearing God, and turning away from evil" (Job 1:1); however, a subterranean taproot of **self-justification** lay concealed deep within him, hidden even from himself! This toxic taproot lodged in Job's DNA lies within each of us, effectively preventing us from maturing further in our relationship with God and sharing together in "all the fullness" of the kingdom. Therefore, in mercy and *jealousy-for* Job, God allowed him to run his full course in '**upward descent**' to expose and violently uproot this impediment of self-justification motivated by self-worth-ship.

"Now when Job's three friends heard of all this adversity that had come upon him, they came…to sympathize with him and comfort him" (Job 2:11). However, these friends were incapable of sympathy and comfort; instead, they could not help accusing (categorizing) Job. Chapters 3-37 essentially read like the transcript of a court-recorder. While being judged unjustly by his friends, Job converted the ash heap upon which he sat into a courtroom, and as an unjust, self-appointed judge, **Job put God on trial to justify himself**.

> Then the Lord answered Job out of the whirlwind [*fusion Vortex of Triune-Agape*]… "Will the **faultfinder** contend with the Almighty [*All-Three-Mighty*]? …**Will you condemn Me that you may be justified?**"… Then Job answered the Lord and said, "…I have heard of You by the hearing of the ear [*e.g. I thought I knew You*]; but now my eye sees You [*Holy, Holy, Holy*]; therefore **I retract** [*all my groundless indictments against You*], and **I repent in dust and ashes** [*e.g. I am a dirtbag filled with Worthless' ashes in dire need of Your grace and re-gene-ration*]" (Job 40:1-8; 42:5-6).

Before Saul was converted into Paul, he was rigorously mentored by the Pharisees and thoroughly acculturated into the most legalistic, categorizing, judgmental, and exacting sect of hypocrites on earth! However, Saul was confronted by "a light brighter than the sun" and heard God in Christ saying, "**I AM Jesus whom you are persecuting** [*e.g. reacting against, executing judgment upon*]" (Acts 9:5). Afterwards, Paul admonished us from personal experience: "You have **no excuse** [*self-justification*], every one of you [*individualists*] who **passes judgment**, for in that [*particular indictment*] which you **judge another**, **you condemn yourself**; for you who **judge** practice the same things [*you are all in the same 'category'*]" (Rom. 2:1). In other words, there is not a solitary human being qualified to judge rightly except the tested, perfected Self-sharing Man Jesus Christ in whom the incorruptible Triune-God resides in fullness.

Dietrich Bonhoeffer, who was imprisoned and executed by the Nazis, received profound insight into the corrupt motivations and grave consequences for those who are unwittingly deputized by "the accuser":

God hates visionary dreaming [*e.g. not from divine in-gen-uity*]; it makes the dreamer proud and pretentious. The man who fashions a visionary ideal of community demands that it be realized by God, by others, and by himself. He enters the community of Christians with his demands, **sets up his own law**, **and**

judges [*categorizes*] **the brethren and God Himself accordingly**. He stands adamant, a living reproach to all others in the circle of brethren. He acts as if he is the creator of the Christian community, **as if his dream binds men together** [*usurping Christ's place as the Nucleus*]. When things do not go his way, he calls the effort a failure. When his ideal picture is destroyed, he sees the community going to smash. So he becomes, first an **accuser of his brethren**, then an **accuser of God**, and finally the despairing **accuser of himself** [*the way of upward descent inevitably dead-ends*] (Bonhoeffer, *Life Together*, Harper & Row, p. 27-28).

To understand further how injustice spreads among corrupt mankind, and the solution our Triune-God has prepared, meditate on Isaiah 59.

7. Distributive Justice

During the years David was in exile, fleeing from King Saul, he became the commander of 600 men. While absent from their camp, a band of raiders carried off all their wives, children, servants, and possessions. David and the 600 pursued these opportunists to recover what was lost; however, 200 men became "too exhausted" to continue and stayed behind "with the baggage." After David and the remaining 400 men overtook the raiders, recovered all that was taken, and returned to the 200, a contention arose that serves as a unique illustration of **God's economy of distributive justice** and how it is implemented:

Then all the wicked and **worthless men** [*lit. sons of Belial*] among those who went with David said, "Because they did not go with us, **we will not give them any of the spoil that we have recovered** [*e.g. by our own self-effort*], except to every man his wife and his children, that they may lead them away and **depart** [*i.e. impetus of relational fission; categorizing the 200 as weak, disowning them as useless*]." Then David said, "**You must not do so, my brothers** [*sons of One: fellow heirs, coequals*], **with what the Lord** [*three Self-sharers*] **has given us**, who has kept us and delivered into our hand the band that came against us [*e.g. it was not our self-effort, but our Triune-God who mercifully recovered our property*].

And who will listen to you [*e.g. eros rationale*] in this matter? For as his **share** is who goes down to the battle, so shall his **share** be who stays by the baggage; **they shall share alike** [*coequally*]." So it has been from that day forward, that he made it **a statute and an ordinance** [*precept of true Triune-Justice*] **for Israel** to this day....David sent some of the spoil to the elders of Judah, to his friends [*coequals*], saying, "Behold, **a gift** [*lit. blessing; e.g. a share*] **for you** from the spoil of the enemies of the Lord" (1 Sam. 30:21-26).

It is truly said, "**There is no honor among thieves**." Raiders, robbers, and confidence-men are certainly thieves, but those who justify confiscating another's property or usurping another's position in a given set of circumstances and even those who simply refuse to share equally are also thieves because they are **opportunists**. Typically, an opportunist joins (*confuses*) with others of like-mind to become one "band" for one calculated purpose: to increase his chances of a payoff for self-gratification. Once any member of his crew has outlived their usefulness, he is disowned or worse! Through the prophet Micah, God expressed His exasperation over man's foolish behavior and counterproductive methods:

Is there yet **a man in the wicked house** [*e.g. an individualist con-fused with other opportunists*], along with **treasures of wickedness** [*e.g. "the mammon of unrighteousness" Luke 16:9*] and a **short measure** [*lit. shrunken ephah*] that is cursed? **Can I** [*three Coequals, Self-sharers*] **justify wicked scales** and a bag of deceptive weights [*withholding and cheating to increase individual profits*]? (Micah 6:10).

To understand the **distributive justice** of God, let's begin by meditating on these comparative proverbs: "Abundant food [*God's provision*] is in the fallow ground of the poor, but it is swept away by **injustice** [*opportunism*]" (Prov. 13:23). "He who oppresses the poor [*in self-exaltation*] taunts his Maker, but he who is gracious to the needy honors Him" (Prov. 14:31). "He who oppresses the poor to make more for himself or who gives to the rich [*e.g. for a calculated payoff*] will only come to poverty" (Prov. 22:16). "He who increases his wealth by interest and usury gathers it for him who is gracious to the poor [*i.e. "the meek…shall inherit the earth"*]" (Prov. 28:8). "Do not rob the poor because he is poor [*vulnerable, defenseless*], or crush the afflicted at the gate [*e.g. rather than receiving them safely inside as coequals*]; for the Lord [*"whose name is 'Jealous'"*] will plead their case and take the life [*lit. rob the soul*] of those who rob them" (Prov. 22:22-23).

Our Triune-God is certainly *spiritual* and "unsearchable" (Rom. 11:33), but at the same time Father, Son, and Spirit are far more *practical* than we imagine: "A just balance and scales belong to the Lord [*e.g. only the three, incorruptible, coequal Self-sharers are capable of distributing equitably*]; all the weights of the bag are His concern" (Prov. 16:11). **Distributive justice** represents all the *practical* ways our Triune-God implements, cultivates, and preserves **coequality** among us. "'Enough, you princes of Israel…stop your **expropriations** from My people,' declares the Lord God. 'You shall have **just balances**, a just ephah and a just bath [*liquid measure*]'" (Ezek. 45:9-10). The Scriptures testify that when believers are led by the Spirit to *practice* distributive justice among the captives of Worthless' world, it is **the most practical, observable, unmistakable sign of the coming of the kingdom of God on the earth**.

> David went and brought up the ark of God [*prophetic type of God in Christ*]...and David was dancing before the Lord with all his might.... When David had finished offering the burnt offering and the peace offering [*Godward priesthood, gene-rosity*], he blessed the people **in the name of the Lord of hosts** [*on behalf of three Self-sharers*]. Further, he **distributed** to all the people, to all the multitude of Israel, both to men and women, a cake of bread and one of dates and one of raisins to each one [*man-ward priesthood, gene-rosity*] (2 Sam. 6:12-19).

The human body of Jesus, "the Son of God," is the prophetic fulfillment of "the ark of God" and now serves as the Nucleus and '**distribution center**' for the superabundant gene-rosity of the Triune-God among mankind:

> For you know the **grace** [*sacrificial Self-sharing*] of our Lord Jesus Christ, that though He was **rich** [*Shareholder, Heir, and Nucleus of*

the *Triune-Dwelling Place*], yet for your sake He became **poor** [*emptied Himself*], so that you through His poverty might become **rich** [*"heirs of God, fellow heirs with Christ"*].... As it is written, **"He scattered abroad, He gave to the poor** [*distributive justice*], His righteousness [*sacrificial Self-sharing Love*] endures forever"** (2 Cor. 8:9; 9:9).

See how God in Christ engaged the multitudes: "Jesus then took the loaves, and having given thanks, He **distributed** to those [*5000*] who were seated; likewise also of the fish as much as they wanted" (John 6:11). The multiplication of the loaves and fish was a natural, practical illustration of Jesus' own *spiritual* gifts, which He distributes **coequally** to each and all the "members" of His one body: "But to each one of us grace was given according to the measure of Christ's [*infinite*] gift. Therefore it says, 'When He ascended on high, He led captive a host of captives [*slaves of Worthless' nature became "slaves of Christ" Eph. 6:6*], and **He gave gifts to men** [*distributive justice*]'" (Eph. 4:7-8).

If you and I are serious about following Jesus and emigrating into the kingdom, we must learn how to gene-rously distribute all we have and all we continue to receive from Him. Jesus answered the rich young ruler, "One thing you still lack [*to fulfill the Law of Agape: sacrificial self-sharing*]; sell all that you possess [*dismantle your autonomous life*] and **distribute** it to the poor [*as coequals*], and you shall have treasure in heaven [*cohabitation of three coequal Self-sharers: three 'Distributors'*]; and come, follow Me [*in downward ascent*]" (Luke 18:22).

On the day of Pentecost, 120 disciples encountered "a mighty rushing wind"—the fusion Vortex of the Trinity came among them for the purpose of distribution: "And there appeared to them **tongues as of fire distributing themselves, and they rested on each one of them** [*coequally*]. And they were all filled with the Spirit…" (Acts 2:2-4). Even now, in this third millennia, these three Eternals are still in the distribution business!

> Now there are varieties of gifts, but the same Spirit. And there are varieties of ministries, and the same Lord. There are varieties of effects, but the same God [*Triune-Agape*] who works all things in all persons [*coequally*]. But to each one is given the manifestation of the Spirit for the common good…. But one and the same Spirit works all these things, **distributing to each one individually** just as He wills [*according to the blueprints of the Trinity*]…. For by one Spirit we were all baptized [*fused*] into one body (1 Cor. 12:7-13).

The secular definition of "**distributive justice**" is the socially equitable and just allocation of goods in a society—how costs and rewards are shared by members of a society. Standards of distributive justice are called "norms." D.R. Forsyth identified "**five basic types of distributive norms: equity, equality, power, need,** and **responsibility**" (Forsyth, D. R.; 2006; *Conflict: Group Dynamics* 5th Ed.; p. 388 – 389; Belmont: CA, Wadsworth, Cengage Learning). Following Forsyth's explanations below, we will look at portions of Scripture that directly address and observe each of these "norms" in appropriate circumstances:

1. Equity: "Member's **outcomes** should be based upon their **inputs**. Therefore, an individual who has invested a large amount of input (e.g. time, money, energy) should receive more from the group than someone who has contributed very little. Members of large groups prefer to base allocations of rewards and costs on equity" (Forsyth). Paul gave the following instructions:

> **Bear one another's burdens**, and thereby fulfill the law of Christ [*Three burden-bearers in one Man lifting and carrying fallen humanity*]. For if anyone thinks he is something when he is nothing, he deceives himself [*buys into Worthless' lie: eros, self-worth-ship*]. But each one must examine **his own work** [*e.g. input*], and then he will have reason for boasting in regard to himself alone, and not in regard to another. For **each one will bear his own load** (Gal. 6:2, 5).

For even when we were with you, we used to give you this order: if anyone is not willing to **work** [*e.g. contribute input*], then he is not to **eat** [*receive output*], either. For we hear that some among you are leading an undisciplined life, **doing no work** [*input*] **at all**, but acting like busybodies [*e.g. pawns of the accuser*]. Now such persons we command and exhort in the Lord Jesus Christ to work in quiet fashion and **eat their own bread**. But as for you, brethren, do not grow weary of **doing good** [*sacrificial self-sharing*] (2 Thess. 3:10).

I [*Paul*] planted, Apollos watered [*e.g. input*], but God was causing the growth [*e.g. output*]. So then neither the one who plants nor the one who waters is anything, but God who causes the growth [*output*]. Now he who plants and he who waters are one [*coequals in relational fusion*]; but **each will receive his own reward** [*output*] **according to his own labor** [*input*] (1 Cor. 3:6-8).

2. Equality: "Regardless of their inputs, all group members should be given an **equal share** of the rewards/costs. Equality supports that someone who contributes 20% of the group's resources should receive as much as someone who contributes 60%" (Forsyth). The Lord instructed Moses, "The rich shall not pay more and the poor shall not pay less than the half shekel, when you give the contribution to the LORD to make atonement for yourselves" (Ex. 30:15). David applied the norm of equality: "For as his share is who goes down to the battle, so shall his share be who stays by the baggage; **they shall share alike**" (1 Sam. 30:24).

Jesus illustrated how the norm of equality is applied in distributive justice in a parable which compares "the kingdom of heaven" to a land-owner hiring laborers over the course of one day. At 7 a.m., the land-owner hired unemployed men who were "standing idle in the marketplace" (see also Luke 7:32); he "agreed with the laborers for a denarius for the day, and sent them into his vineyard." Later, at 9 a.m. he found others standing idle and hired them also. At noon and at 3 p.m. and 5 p.m. he returned and hired others still waiting there.

> When evening came, the owner of the vineyard said to his foreman, "Call the laborers and pay them their wages, **beginning with the last group to the first**." When those hired about the eleventh hour came, each one received a denarius [*one day's wage*]. When those hired first came, **they thought they would receive more**; but each of them also received a denarius. When they received it they grumbled at the landowner, saying, "These men have worked only one hour [*minimal input*], and **you have made them equal to us** who have

borne the burden and the scorching heat of the day." But he answered, "Friend, I am doing you no wrong; did you not agree with me for a denarius? Take what is yours and go, but **I wish to give to this last man the same as to you** [*coequally*]. Is it not lawful for me to do what I wish with what is my own? Or is your eye **envious** because I am **generous?**" So **the last shall be first, and the first last** (Matt. 20:1-16).

3. Power: "Those with more authority, status, or control over the group should receive more than those in lower level positions" (Forsyth). Instead of the term *power*, we might call this **invested authority**. Paul instructed Timothy, "The elders who rule well are to be considered **worthy of double honor, especially those who work hard** at preaching and teaching. For the Scripture says, 'You shall not muzzle the ox while he is threshing,' and 'The laborer is worthy of his wages'" (1 Tim. 5:1-18). Here, we must consider another example: as the Governor of Israel, **Nehemiah** could "lawfully" collect material and human resources from his constituents to supply his own need and comfort, yet he **refused the benefits of his authority** because he **answered to a higher law—coequality in Agape**:

From the day that I was appointed to be their governor in the land of Judah…for twelve years, neither I nor my kinsmen have eaten **the governor's food allowance**. But the former governors who were before me laid burdens on the people and took from them bread and wine besides forty shekels of silver; even their servants domineered the people. But I did not do so because of **the fear of God** [*e.g. I worth-ship and serve three sacrificial Self-sharers*] (Neh. 5:14-19).

4. Need: "Those in greatest need should be provided with resources needed to meet those needs. These individuals should be given more resources than those who already possess them, regardless of their input" (Forsyth). Among the first church, "there was not a **needy** person among them, for all who were **owners** of land or houses would sell them and bring the proceeds of the sales and lay them at the apostles' feet, and they would be **distributed to each** [*coequally*] **as any had need**" (Acts 4:34–35). John the Baptist warned the people of Israel:

"Bear fruits [*sacrificial self-sharing*] in keeping with repentance [*forsaking self-worth-ship*].... Indeed the axe is already laid at the root of the trees; so every tree that does not bear good fruit [*reciprocal gene-rosity*] is cut down and thrown into the fire." And the crowds were questioning him, saying, "Then what shall we do?" And he would answer and say to them,

"The man who has two tunics is to share with him who has none; and he who has food is to do likewise [*e.g. distributive justice*]" (Luke 3:8-11).

5. Responsibility: "Group members who have the most should share their resources with those who have less" (Forsyth). Paul wrote:

For if the readiness [*to sacrificially share*] is present, it is acceptable according to what a person has, not according to what he does not have. For this is not for the ease of others and for your affliction, but **by way of equality** [*the law of Father, Son, Spirit*]—at this present time **your abundance being a supply for their need**, so that their abundance also may become a supply for your need [*reciprocal generosity: kingdom economics*], **that there may be equality** [Trinity-likeness], as it is written, "He who gathered much did not have too much [*self-indulgence*], and he who gathered little had no lack [*famine*]" (2 Cor. 8:12-15).

The Scriptures affirm that in various circumstances, each of these five norms outlined by Forsyth—equity, equality, power (invested authority), need, responsibility—is an appropriate approach to true justice. Yet, **misapplied, any of these norms can also bring injustice in the name of justice!** For example, "You shall not follow the masses in doing evil [*majority opinion of what is right/just*], nor shall you testify in a dispute so as to turn aside after a multitude [*e.g. popular opinion/political correctness*] in order to **pervert justice**, nor shall you be **partial to** [*lit. honor*] **a poor man** in his dispute [*simply because he is poor*]" (Ex. 23:2-3). Living in Ukraine and Uganda since 2000, we have seen firsthand that the poor are not automatically right: "A poor man who oppresses the lowly is like a driving rain that leaves no food" (Prov. 28:3).

In many cases, *Affirmative Action* has over-shot its target of achieving racial representation, integration, and equality in the workplace. Though the idea is noble, it is not the *proactive* intervention of God's justice, but a *reactionary*, man-made invention implemented by corruptible individualists and executed with partiality. Regardless of how well-conceived and comprehensive a plan of distributive justice may seem, or how conscientiously it may appear to be executed, it will not and cannot provide *gen-uine* **coequality** and *true* fairness if it is rooted in anything other than Agape: "And if I give all my possessions to feed the poor…but do not have *Agape* [*sacrificial self-sharing Love*] it profits me nothing" (1 Cor. 13:3). There is a vast difference between true justice and man's justice:

> **Dispense true** [*Trinity-like*] **justice** and practice kindness and compassion each to his

brother [*e.g. coequality is the fruit of reciprocal self-sharing*]; and do not oppress the widow or the orphan, the stranger or the poor; and do not devise evil [*eros calculation, opportunism*] in your hearts against one another (Zech. 7:9-10).

Ultimately, the Spirit must indicate to us which of these five norms of distributive justice comes to bear in each, specific situation. Each unique human being and the times, circumstances, and interactions in which we find ourselves in our daily lives are all dynamic variables that require the Spirit to apply the coequality and justice of our Triune-God. The Spirit "searches all things, even the depths of God" (1 Cor. 2:10), and the Spirit of Christ is "able to judge the thoughts and intentions of the heart" (Heb. 4:12); therefore, He is able to show us how the law of Agape may be properly applied, coequality preserved, and justice fulfilled among all who are involved.

Agape is not a **static** set of laws, but a **living Triune-dynamic** that must be seen, heard, observed, and applied in responsive obedience! Paul made our mandate clear:

Therefore, **be imitators of God** [*three Coequals: an "Us" in fusion oneness*], as beloved **children** [*an 'us' in fusion oneness*], and **walk in Agape** [*coequality*], just as **Christ** also loved us and gave Himself up *for* us [*e.g. to receive* *us into His own body as coequal "members"*], an offering and a sacrifice [*of one, many-membered, Trinity-like Man*] to God as a fragrant aroma (Eph. 5:1-2).

In conclusion, Triune-Justice has been revealed and demonstrated in and through the Man Jesus to provide a living Standard of individual **integrity** (godliness) that facilitates relational, inter-personal **integration** (Trinity-like fusion) and prevents relational **disintegration** (fission). The Scriptures describe the cohabitation of the kingdom of God as **one shared estate** comprised of the unlocked, adjoining gardens of our individual lives (see Luke 13:18-19; 17:21; Song 4:12; Acts 4:32). Embracing *The Equalizer* and embracing one another as **coequals** together "in Him" enables us to respect one another's gardens—not to forcibly enter the garden of another with '**entitlement**' to take, control, or abuse but rather to enter bearing gifts to add to their garden, to build one shared estate, and to cultivate one shared life.

Perhaps this sheds light on Jesus' observation, "the kingdom of heaven suffers violence [*lit. is forcibly entered*] and violent men [*i.e. religious opportunists*] take it by force [*lit. seize it for themselves*]" (Matt. 11:12). When I am invited into the garden of another, I must enter as a **sacrificial self-sharer** to celebrate their individuality, to respect their freedom, and to lay down my own life for my friend. In other words, Justice is the gift our Triune-God has given to each and all of us 'porcupines' to keep us warm in one shared burrow!

Our study of "the Lord is a God of justice" will continue in the next *Plumbline*, subtitled *Encountering the Equalizer*, which includes these themes:

Setting Earth on the Pillar of Justice

Preserving Freedom and Coequality

The Equalizer
"Jesus called them to Himself"
Exposing 'Even-steven'
Jesus Out-socialists the Socialists
Judged Through a Man

P.O. Box 3709 ❖ Cookeville, TN 38502
931.520.3730 ❖ lc@lifechangers.org

CPSIA information can be obtained at www.ICGtesting.com
Printed in the USA
LVOW10s0046230316

480351LV00002B/2/P